ANCHORED IN GRACE

Fixed Points for Humble Faith

Jeremy Walker
Cruciform Press | June 2015

To my dear children,
so eager for Daddy to write,
with the earnest prayer that each one
might come to be anchored in grace.

CruciformPress

"Rarely does the title of a book so clearly represent its contents as does *Anchored in Grace: Fixed Points for Humble Faith*, by Jeremy Walker. With brevity and precision, Walker sets forth God's work of salvation in the believer from beginning to end. In a day when there is so much confusion regarding even the most fundamental truths of redemption, this concise yet comprehensive work is a clear beacon of light to guide the seeker and to instruct and comfort the believer."

Paul David Washer, Director, HeartCry Missionary Society

"As a pastor I am always looking for a book that is brief, simple, and biblical in its presentation of the God-exalting doctrines of grace to put into the hands of believers. I think my search is now over! In *Anchored in Grace: Fixed Points for Humble Faith* Jeremy Walker provides us with a book that shows us in small compass how God's grace has turned wretched sinners into heaven-bound saints. Wonderful!"

Conrad Mbewe, Pastor, Kabwata Baptist Church; Chancellor, African Christian University, Lusaka, Zambia

"Crisp, clear, concise, and biblical, Walker's book offers up the doctrines of God's grace in a manner persuasive to the mind and powerful to the heart."

Dr. Joel R. Beeke, President, Puritan Reformed Theological Seminary, Grand Rapids, Michigan

"A sure-footed journey through the doctrines of grace — foundational truths for godliness and discipleship — by a trusted guide. Reading this book will both thrill and convict, challenge and confirm. Essential reading for discipleship groups, Adult Sunday School classes, and individuals determined to grow in grace. Warmly recommended."

Derek W. H. Thomas, Senior Minister, First Presbyterian Church, Columbia SC; The Robert Strong Professor of Systematic and Pastoral Theology, Reformed Theological Seminary, Atlanta

"Don't miss out on reading this book. If you have been a Christian for forty years or more you will find it fresh and faith-enhancing. If you are a new follower of Jesus Christ and see the faith as a collection of wonderful pieces of a jigsaw but have not yet seen the overall plan of God fitting them all together, then this is the book for you. Here is God's plan for the individual Christian, for the whole church, and for the message to be preached from every pulpit. Read it! Think about what you are reading. It is the way to joy and peace in the Christian life and also the means of achieving your chief end in life, glorifying God and enjoying him forever."

Geoff Thomas, minister for fifty years in Alfred Place Baptist Church, Aberystwyth, Wales

"This is a meaty feast of solid doctrinal truth crammed into a short, pointed, and applied book. The deeply encouraging doctrines of grace are opened up to us and explained clearly. Each of the five chapters has helpful application points to finish. There is nothing new here for the mature believer, nor should there be. That's why I love it. This is historical, biblical truth brought back into the light for the modern Christian. For the new believer, however, this will be a great opening introduction into the beautifully God-honoring doctrines of God's glorious grace. Everyone's a winner with this one."

Mez McConnell, author; Pastor, Niddrie Community Church, Edinburgh; founder and director, 20schemes

"Everything Jeremy Walker writes moves me to love my Savior more. So you can imagine this book, *Anchored In Grace,* which speaks of the foundational truths of our salvation in Jesus, is certainly no exception. Through Jeremy's unique and compelling writing style, you will experience both the weighty realities of our daily need for Jesus, and yet the soaring freedoms these same truths provide. Read this book and allow the never-ending river of God's grace bound in these pages to wash you afresh."

Brian Croft, pastor, author, founder of Practical Shepherding

Cruciform Press

Books of about 100 pages
Clear, inspiring, gospel-centered

We like to keep it simple. So we publish short, clear, useful, inexpensive books for Christians and other curious people. Books that make sense and are easy to read, even as they tackle serious subjects.

We do this because the good news of Jesus Christ—the gospel—is the only thing that actually explains why this world is so wonderful and so awful all at the same time. Even better, the gospel applies to every single area of life, and offers real answers that aren't available from any other source.

These are books you can afford, enjoy, finish easily, benefit from, and remember. Check us out and see. Then join us as part of a publishing revolution that's good news for the gospel, the church, and the world.

CruciformPress.com

Anchored in Grace: Fixed Truths for Humble Faith

Print / PDF ISBN: 978-1-941114-04-9
ePub ISBN: 978-1-941114-06-3
Mobipocket ISBN: 978-1-941114-05-6

Table of Contents

Introduction 7

One   *Fallen*................................ 11
Who Needs to Be Saved?

Two   *Chosen* 25
On What Basis Are We Saved?

Three   *Redeemed*............................. 43
How Is This Salvation Accomplished?

Four   *Called* 57
How Do We Come to Possess
the Blessings of Salvation?

Five   *Enduring* 71
How Do We Remain in Christ to the End?

Author 93
Endnotes 93

Excerpts: *Who Am I?* by Jerry Bridges...... 94
More from Cruciform Press 102

INTRODUCTION

In his great treatment of spiritual warfare, *The Christian in Complete Armour*, William Gurnall speaks of what he calls "catechize-points." These, he says, are "truths necessary to be known and believed."[1] The truths upon which I wish to focus in this short book provide us with a stunning display of grace. They are truths which with Christians need to be thoroughly acquainted, truths with which pastors must thoroughly acquaint the people whom they serve. These are the paths to walk so that you do not miss your way to heaven, nor fail to honor the Lord God along the way. These are the anchors of the faith that mature Christians need to point out to the generations following us. These are spiritual realities to reckon with. These are the gospel verities that must be defended against the errors and heresies that repeatedly threaten to undermine or overwhelm them, either by force or by fraud.

These are central truths. They cannot be pushed to one side or downplayed without restricting our views of God and twisting our views of self. They are determinative, in large measure, for our views of Christian experience, life, duty, and joy. They help to define our gospel witness as the church of Jesus Christ. Get these wrong and so much else will be immediately and persistently skewed.

These are humbling truths. They strip away the boasting to which proud and rebellious man is inclined. With searing honesty they make us face the facts about our own sinful hearts, our spiritual need, and our utter dependence on the mercies and favors of God acting freely and graciously in accordance with his glorious character and infinite being. They are truths that necessarily empty us of self before they fill us with Christ.

These are saving truths. These things are the ground of our hope. Fail to reckon with these things and there is no deliverance for our souls and bodies. Again, there is a holy progression and a divine logic at work. Like a sick man, we must acknowledge the disease in order to pursue the physician. We must accept the diagnosis in order to obtain the medicine. With regard to our souls, we will not flee to Christ as Savior until we are brought to acknowledge the salvation we need as found in him alone. Then, and only then, do we run to him and hide ourselves in him and find all our joy.

These are comforting truths. Here the soul— however stained or troubled in itself, however weak and feeble we know ourselves to be or fear ourselves to be, whatever challenges and obstacles we face, whatever trials and temptations lie before us—finds all that it will ever need. Here and here only we can rest in peace.

Finally, these are God-glorifying truths. They exalt God in Christ. They make much of him, they draw attention to his person, and they shed light upon his work. Here his being and his doing are made manifest. Nowhere outside of salvation through the Lamb do we find such a high and clear revelation of who God is and what God is like. Here the glory of God shines in his grace as nowhere else, prompting lives of earnest service and songs of ardent praise.

My intention is simply to survey some of these fundamental truths—God's display of his grace—in order that we might feel their sweet force for ourselves. In each instance, I will take what might be called an "epitomizing text"— a short portion of God's Word that encapsulates something of the truth in question. I hope to demonstrate that it is by no means the only Scripture that proves the point, and so bring to bear something of the whole counsel of God upon the matter. My concern is both to explain and to apply these truths. My intention is not first polemical. However, I trust that as we see these truths springing from the pages of our Bibles they will be persuasive to direct, confirm, and encourage us in the things God has revealed. We must see that these are not dead letters, but spiritual realities that ought to grip our souls and govern our thoughts and deeds.

In so doing, I trust we shall be instructed, humbled, saved, and comforted, and bring glory and honor to the God of our salvation as he holds before us in his Word a display of his grace in Christ Jesus, his Son and our Savior.

One
FALLEN

Who Needs to Be Saved?

What then? Are we better than they? Not at all.
For we have previously charged both Jews and
Greeks that they are all under sin. As it is written:
"There is none righteous, no, not one; there is
none who understands; there is none who seeks
after God. They have all turned aside; they have
together become unprofitable; there is none who
does good, no, not one." (Romans 3:9–12)

We must begin with our condition as *fallen* creatures,
what the Scottish pastor and theologian Thomas Boston
called "the state of nature."[2] This is a vital first step
because if we make a false diagnosis of our condition
then we will seek out flawed remedies and accept false
answers. To do so in this instance would be fatal.

In order to make a proper assessment of this matter,
we shall trace out two strands of evidence. The primary
and fundamental strand is the testimony of God's
Word. The secondary and supplementary strand is the

evidence of the world around us. Having surveyed the evidence, we shall then draw out some particular inferences and conclusions.

Evidence: The Testimony of Scripture

The testimony of Scripture must be, for Christians, the defining truth. This is where we begin seeking a final answer to every question addressed therein. What does the Word of God say about the human heart? What does the Bible reveal about our natural state or fallen condition? It describes it in various terms.

Deadness. Scripture describes our natural condition as one of *deadness*. Paul concludes part of his reasoning with the Roman Christians by telling them that, "therefore, just as through one man sin entered the world, and death through sin, and thus death spread to all men, because all sinned" (Romans 5:12). Paul traces our condition to its fountain in the sin of Adam. All mankind, descending from Adam by ordinary generation, sinned in him and fell with him in his first transgression. All our sinning is traced back to the sinful nature we inherited from our first father. Ours is an hereditary condition, and a dreadful one. Everyone, Christian or otherwise, is by nature "dead in trespasses and sins" (Ephesians 2:1). Death—spiritual death—is revealed by our pattern of existence marked by trespasses and sins. It is a state of spiritual inertness, or utter spiritual lifelessness.

Rebellion. The Bible also describes our condition as one of *rebellion*. Again, writing to the Romans, Paul says that "the carnal mind is enmity against God; for it is not subject to the law of God, nor indeed can be" (Romans 8:7). We exist, by nature, in a state of hostility toward God, neither willing nor able to live in accordance with his holy law. In ourselves, it must be said of us as it was of many Jews in Christ's day, "you are of your father the devil, and the desires of your father you want to do" (John 8:44). It is the devil's falsehoods we believe and his will we embrace, while rejecting God's truth and God's will (Ephesians 2:2).

Enslavement. Again, the Scriptures describe us as in a state of *enslavement*. Jesus makes it an axiomatic principle that "whoever commits sin is a slave of sin" (John 8:34). That is, a life marked by persistent, thoroughgoing, unrepentant sin is the life of man enslaved to sin. Paul similarly personifies lusts when writing to Titus. He looks back with sorrow, describing how "we ourselves were also once foolish, disobedient, deceived, serving various lusts and pleasures, living in malice and envy, hateful and hating one another" (Titus 3:3).

The apostle also describes those who do not yet know the truth as trapped in "the snare of the devil, having been taken captive by him to do his will" (2 Timothy 2:26). Our sins are the devil's snares, means by which he brings us into his vicious captivity. He is our fierce and heartless foe, who loves to have us under his oppressive and destructive government.

The behavior of the unconverted man or woman reveals that our fallen desires are our cruel masters. We are as bound to commit sin as water is to flow downhill.

Blindness and deafness. Further, we are described in terms of spiritual *blindness and deafness*. We see but do not perceive; we hear but do not understand (Mark 4:12). Our best and most brilliant thinkers, even those who consider themselves theologians, if left to their own wisdom, are blind leaders of the blind, so that both fall into the ditch (Luke 6:39). We have no spiritual sense and awareness by nature.

Inability. Again, there is a horrible *inability* in us: "the natural man does not receive the things of the Spirit of God, for they are foolishness to him; nor can he know them, because they are spiritually discerned" (1 Corinthians 2:14). The truth of God is "foolishness" to the natural man. Despite some sense of eternity, he lacks the spiritual discernment to grasp truly spiritual — we might properly say, Spiritual — things. He lacks the capacity to know better and acts accordingly:

> This I say, therefore, and testify in the Lord, that you should no longer walk as the rest of the Gentiles walk, in the futility of their mind, having their understanding darkened, being alienated from the life of God, because of the ignorance that is in them, because of the blindness of their heart; who, being past feeling, have given themselves over to lewdness, to work all uncleanness with greediness. (Ephesians 4:17–19)

Indeed, even if he could see the way, he does not have the ability to do what is acceptable to God: "those who are in the flesh cannot please God" (Romans 8:8). Jeremiah asks the question that traps every sinner. "Can the Ethiopian change his skin or the leopard its spots? Then may you also do good who are accustomed to do evil" (Jeremiah 13:23). Christ himself makes clear the inability of the unresponsive heart of the sinner to move toward God: "No one can come to Me unless the Father who sent Me draws him; and I will raise him up at the last day" (John 6:44).

Sinfulness. This whole description is rooted in the reality of *sinfulness*. Here is the root of the matter. We are sinners by nature, "brought forth in iniquity" and conceived in sin (Psalm 51:5). The entire human race stands under the divine indictment that "the LORD saw that the wickedness of man was great in the earth, and that every intent of the thoughts of his heart was only evil continually" (Genesis 6:5). Our transgression is thoroughly instinctive, for "the wicked are estranged from the womb; they go astray as soon as they are born, speaking lies" (Psalm 58:3). Those words describe both the root and the fruit of our condition. Lawlessness is woven into our hearts (1 John 3:4) and lawless deeds result. Christ shows the horror of such hearts, even while the outward man might be carrying out deeds of extravagant religiosity:

Not everyone who says to Me, "Lord, Lord," shall

enter the kingdom of heaven, but he who does the will of My Father in heaven. Many will say to Me in that day, "Lord, Lord, have we not prophesied in Your name, cast out demons in Your name, and done many wonders in Your name?" And then I will declare to them, "I never knew you; depart from Me, you who practice lawlessness!" (Matthew 7:21–23)

Such is the consistent, almost relentless, testimony of Scripture. We are by nature dead, rebellious, enslaved, senseless, incapable sinners. It is an awful but an honest portrait of the unconverted heart.

Evidence: The Testimony of Daily Life

While the testimony of the Word of God should be sufficient for the Christian, we may also expect experience to bear out what we read there. In truth, if we survey the world with the same honesty with which we face the Bible, we do find this to be the case.

<u>Children.</u> We can see it, for example, in the *behavior of children*. As any candid parent will tell you, no one needs to teach a toddler selfishness or greed or anger. No one must school a child in deceit or pride. But there cannot be many parents who set out to develop sin in their children. Nevertheless, in the face of the best human efforts, the blithest little baby allowed to develop in the most neutral or positive environment will soon enough produce the fruit of a fallen nature.

The world. Or consider, more generally, *the state of the world*. As I write there are wars being fought out in Ukraine, Syria, Iraq, Afghanistan, and countless other places around the world. By the time you read these words, those wars may well have been won and lost by respective sides, with all the resultant misery. Other conflicts will be simmering or boiling over in other parts of the planet, and you will be able to list them for yourselves. But you need not look so far afield. Walk the streets of your village, town, or city with your eyes and ears open. Do you see some rural idyll or scenes of metropolitan bliss? Or do you not find, more or less evidently, the marks of man's iniquity scorched into countless lives? Do the sins and sorrows of this world contradict or illustrate the truth of God's Word?

Your heart. Then think of *your own heart*. Has God given you any accurate and honest insight into the state of your own soul? If he has, then you will confess that the portrait of the suspect sketched by the Word of God matches your inner man. The Bible has delineated with painful accuracy the modes and moods of your soul. By nature, apart from God, you think the way a fallen man thinks, you speak the way a fallen man speaks, you feel the way a fallen man feels, you act the way a fallen man acts. You lift your eyes and look into the mirror of the Scriptures, and you see yourself as you really are. It is not a pretty sight.

Gospel resistance. Consider, too, the *characteristic resistance to the gospel* that lies in our hearts. It is played out in the antagonism sinners have to the good news. It manifests itself in denials of the principles the gospel lays out and derision for the responses the gospel demands. The message of the cross—that Jesus of Nazareth, who was God's Son and God's Christ, suffered and died according to the Scriptures, being crucified in the place of the ungodly, rising again on the third day, and that only through faith in him can we be made right with God—is foolishness to every unenlightened heart. The notion that such a despicable or deluded individual (if we acknowledge his historical validity) dying such a disgusting death (if we permit that it was no fraud or inaccuracy of record) is somehow required in order for a sinner (if we acknowledge ourselves to be such) to stand acquitted of his guilt (on the assumption that there is some standard by which we are judged) before a holy God (if we allow the idea of his existence to stand) offends the natural mind. It is foolishness to those who have made human reason their idol and a stumbling block to those who imagine themselves good enough for anything that may be required of them. For many, despite the most careful explanations and the most earnest entreaties, they are swift to despise it, ready to dismiss it, and remain utterly inert in the face of it.

A Universal Condition

When we face these strands of evidence, we are obliged to use the language of universality and totality:

What then? Are we better than they? Not at all. For we have previously charged both Jews and Greeks that they are all under sin. As it is written: "There is none righteous, no, not one; there is none who understands; there is none who seeks after God. They have all turned aside; they have together become unprofitable; there is none who does good, no, not one."...Now we know that whatever the law says, it says to those who are under the law, that every mouth may be stopped, and all the world may become guilty before God. (Romans 3:9–12, 19)

All we like sheep have gone astray; we have turned—every one—to his own way; and the LORD has laid on Him the iniquity of us all. (Isaiah 53:6)

Even addressing those who have come to know the blessings of Christ's saving work, God's spokesmen remind us that we too were once entirely subject to sin. It is clear that the whole humanity of all humanity is subject to the taint of sin. To put it another way, every part of the whole life and every element of the whole person of every human being demonstrates our true natural condition as alienated from and antagonistic to God.

All the faculties and capacities of every human creature are under the same condemnation. Our fundamental and pervasive character is one of moral evil. We are morally and ethically disordered at every point of our being. Our minds and hearts are darkened. Our affections and emotions are twisted. Our wills and desires are perverted. Our consciences are dull and inaccurate. Our bodies themselves lead us astray.

This is not to suggest that no one can be saved from such a state. We shall come in due course to consider the remedy provided for mankind dead in trespasses and sins.

Neither is everyone is as bad as they could be. That would be to suggest a sort of absolute depravity. In the middle film of Christopher Nolan's Batman trilogy, *The Dark Knight* (2008), we are faced with the profoundly unsettling portrayal of a villain named the Joker. When the film first came out, many Christian critics were quite happy to turn to the Joker as a portrayal of what is sometimes called total depravity. But the Joker portrays something closer to this absolute depravity, described by the actor who played him as a "psychopathic, mass-murdering, schizophrenic clown with zero empathy."[3] That may be a potential manifestation of depravity, but it is not a common or "normal" one, nor is it what the Bible has primarily in mind when it speaks of the corruption of the whole nature. The little old lady with the blue rinse who may live next door is as much subject to this corruption as the most violent criminal imaginable. What differs is the expression of the condition.

Simply put, we are all sinners through and through.

We are all sinners by nature and deed. Every human being is thoroughly corrupt, that corruption being total in its extent if not in its degree. Every one of us is naturally subject to a comprehensive spiritual deadness that afflicts the whole human race.

Taking Stock

What shall we make of this? What inferences and conclusions must we draw?

Realism. First of all, there should be *realism* about those who are, at this point in time, unconverted — those who are not true Christians. Such men and women, boys and girls, must be born again: "Most assuredly, I say to you, unless one is born of water and the Spirit, he cannot enter the kingdom of God. That which is born of the flesh is flesh, and that which is born of the Spirit is spirit. Do not marvel that I said to you, 'You must be born again'" (John 3:5–7). This is not the language of obligation (it is not a command) but of an absolute spiritual necessity. No one moves to God, or even desires to move toward God, without God moving first to draw that one to himself. We may and should mourn over the hardness of men's hearts, but it should not surprise us. In fact, we are told to expect it. When believers take the gospel into the world, they take it to those who are utterly dead in themselves. We must be realistic about that and about what it means for the hostile reception that the unregenerate heart will give to both the message and messengers of the cross.

We must be realistic, no less, about our own children, if we are Christians. We cannot excuse or ameliorate their sin. All their privileges growing up under the gospel, all the healthful influences brought to bear upon them, do not in themselves render our children less sinful.

Honesty. Furthermore, there must be *honesty* concerning our own condition. It may be that even now the Holy Spirit is using this chapter to give some reader, perhaps for the first time, a clearer understanding of the evil of your nature, the criminality of your record, the rebellion of your heart. Have you grasped that, as you are or were, there is no good thing in you or from you? That might be a dawning realization for a Christian who has never considered these things before. It might even be a revelation of your present utter lostness and your deadness to your own dead state. If that is so, do you see that you need a Savior? Do you now understand that from the womb you have gone astray? We must face the facts.

Soberness. It should mean *soberness* regarding the sanctification of a Christian. I am referring to the gradual process by which a saved sinner is made more and more like Jesus Christ. When we are saved there is radical change — the root of our humanity is made new. In Christ, we are new creations: the old has passed away, all things have become new (2 Corinthians 5:17). In Christ, the whole tenor and direction of the Christian's life changes. This is a wonder of divine grace. But our whole humanity needs addressing. That new life at the core of our being needs to be increasingly worked out in all our faculties and capacities. That means a battle on every front, for sin has had a more or less free rein on every front, and now needs to be reined in, ridden down, and rooted out. Where sin reigned, righteousness must replace it, being cultivated in thought and word and deed. Everywhere that sin had its expression, a holy counterpart must now be established and advanced. Let there be no illusions about the extent and degree of the work required and of the time and effort that may—under God—be required to advance the believer's real holiness.

Conviction. Faced with this reality, there should be a *conviction* that nothing less than divine power and wisdom are required to bring life from death. Only the almightiness of God can bring light into such darkness. Only the Lord can change our nature and reverse our spiritual polarity. There is no remedy for sinners dead in their trespasses and sins other than the power and wisdom of God as they are revealed in Jesus Christ and him crucified.

Humility. There must, then, be *humility* concerning our salvation. There is no mere human being who can make any contribution toward our right standing with God. In its initial acts, salvation is all of the divine prerogative. In its subsequent processes, even our actions depend on and respond to God's prior acts. The renewed heart, with all its gracious operations, finds its origin in the sovereign grace of God. Salvation is accomplished outside of us and granted and applied to us. Salvation is given to us as those who are dead and desperate. All the glory and honor of salvation therefore belong to its Giver. Believers are blessed, and God alone is the Benefactor.

Earnestness. This ought to lead to *earnestness* in prayer for the powerful operations of the Holy Spirit. If men are indeed so dead in themselves, and if any and all believers made alive are so entirely dependent upon God, then how much ought we to be in prayer to the Spirit of God, who grants life in Christ! How much should we be pleading that he would come in sweet and saving power to open the eyes of the inwardly blind, to unstop the ears of the spiritually deaf, to give life to those who are dead in sin. Salvation is of the Lord. We must therefore look to him to give it, and plead with him to grant it.

Thankfulness. Finally, let there be abundant *thankfulness* for divine grace. Salvation *is* of the Lord! That being so, all honor and glory belong to him alone. If anyone is saved—if you or I are saved—then the origin of the whole and the source of every part is found ultimately in God who redeems. The accomplishment of salvation and the application of salvation are acts and works of free and sovereign grace. Praise the God of our salvation, Father, Son, and Spirit!

Two
CHOSEN

On What Basis Are We Saved?

*Blessed be the God and Father of our Lord Jesus
Christ, who has blessed us with every spiritual
blessing in the heavenly places in Christ, just
as He chose us in Him before the foundation of
the world, that we should be holy and without
blame before Him in love, having predestined
us to adoption as sons by Jesus Christ to Himself,
according to the good pleasure of His will, to the
praise of the glory of His grace, by which He made
us accepted in the Beloved. (Ephesians 1:3–6)*

If we drew only one conclusion from the first
chapter, I trust it would be something along these lines:
for men and women like us, by nature being dead in
our trespasses and sins, the only possible solution or
remedy lies outside mankind. It must, of necessity, lie
with God alone.

We can put it another way, in the form of a question.
If everyone by nature deserves death and hell, how is it

that some obtain life and heaven? If someone has those blessings, where did they come from and how did that person come by them? The beginning of the answer to that question is addressed in the first chapter of Paul's letter to the Ephesians, as well as in a number of other places.

The answer is essentially this: if you have spiritual life in you, it is because you were *chosen*. This is the second "catechize-point"—to use Gurnall's language again—that we must address. Here is another spiritual reality to reckon with, another anchor point for our faith. We will take Ephesians 1:3–6 as our starting point, drawing in other texts from God's Word as appropriate.

> Blessed be the God and Father of our Lord Jesus Christ, who has blessed us with every spiritual blessing in the heavenly places in Christ, just as He chose us in Him before the foundation of the world, that we should be holy and without blame before Him in love, having predestined us to adoption as sons by Jesus Christ to Himself, according to the good pleasure of His will, to the praise of the glory of His grace, by which He made us accepted in the Beloved.

Salvation Involves a Choice

It should be immediately clear from the language of the Bible that salvation involves a choice. The plain sense of Paul's language in these words written to the church in Ephesus is of selection, of choosing, of gathering out. The apostle is entering into a thankful survey of the blessings of salvation. Here at the front end is this grand declaration of an act of deliberate and personal selection of some from among many. The Ephesians — and, by extension all other believers — enjoy spiritual blessings in the heavenlies because they were chosen to them. Our Lord Jesus says as much when he tells his disciples, "if you were of the world, the world would love its own. Yet because you are not of the world, but I chose you out of the world, therefore the world hates you" (John 15:19).

Who Chooses?

It is God who chooses. Election, while not excluding the Trinity considered as the three in one, is here distinctly described as an act of God the Father: "Blessed be the God and Father of our Lord Jesus Christ..." You will notice it is definitely God the Father who chose us. The initiative, intent, power, and accomplishment of this choice lie with God and are exercised toward "us." Although we are not addressing in full at this point the issue of our responses to this choice, it is clear that this choosing is a divine act, not a human one. When Paul refers to it elsewhere, he tells the Thessalonian Christians that he knows, "beloved brethren, your election by God" (1 Thessalonians 1:4). In this matter of selection, the Christian was essentially passive, operated upon rather than operating.

Who Are Chosen?

Who, then, are the "us" who are chosen? As already
indicated, they are ones selected out of a great number.
Specifically, in terms of the letter in question, the chosen
ones can now be called "the saints who are in Ephesus,
and faithful in Christ Jesus" (Ephesians 1:1). They were
not so before they were chosen; they have become so
by virtue of their choosing and the acts that followed on
from it. If we read the book of the Acts, we see the kind
of people the Ephesians were by nature. Their portrait
emerges in chapters eighteen and nineteen of that history,
which you may read at your leisure. They were part of
and enmeshed in a society marked by idolatry, sorcery,
and carnality. They answered entirely to the description of fallen humanity sketched out in the first chapter
of this book. Indeed, in the second chapter of the letter,
Paul summarizes their past state in the bluntest language:

> And you He made alive, who were dead in
> trespasses and sins, in which you once walked
> according to the course of this world, according
> to the prince of the power of the air, the spirit who
> now works in the sons of disobedience, among
> whom also we all once conducted ourselves in the
> lusts of our flesh, fulfilling the desires of the flesh
> and of the mind, and were by nature children of
> wrath, just as the others…. Therefore remember
> that you, once Gentiles in the flesh—who are
> called Uncircumcision by what is called the Cir-

cumcision made in the flesh by hands—that at that time you were without Christ, being aliens from the commonwealth of Israel and strangers from the covenants of promise, having no hope and without God in the world. But now in Christ Jesus you who once were far off have been brought near by the blood of Christ.... Now, therefore, you are no longer strangers and foreigners, but fellow citizens with the saints and members of the household of God." (Ephesians 2:1–3, 11–13, 19)

Paul is now writing to some who belonged to that great mass of sinful people. However, some were chosen, and by virtue of that choice can now be described as saints and faithful (Ephesians 1:1). Those who were not a people can now be described as the people of God (1 Peter 2:9–10).

And what is true specifically of this letter's recipients is true generally of all and any who are chosen. The letter to the Ephesians offers a representative microcosm of the people of God considered in any time and place.

In Whom Were They Chosen?

They were chosen "in Christ." This divine choice is made in connection with Christ with regard to his person and his work. It carries us back into the realm of the divine determination to save, into the inner workings of what many have called the covenant of grace. It gives us glimpses into the heavenly compact that lies behind all God's gracious dealings with those whom he saves.

Indeed, any choice of us apart from our being in Christ would be self-defeating, an empty intention and failing promise, for all the substance of blessing entailed in God's choice of us is secured by and obtained in Christ. It is not possible to know or enjoy any saving kindnesses outside of or apart from Christ. Even the appointment of salvation is bound up with him. We were chosen in connection with Christ the Son of God.

When Were They Chosen?

Those who have been chosen were chosen "before the foundation of the world." What a marvel! This choice was made before even the world was! As the apostle says to the church in Thessalonica, "we are bound to give thanks to God always for you, brethren beloved by the Lord, because God from the beginning chose you for salvation through sanctification by the Spirit and belief in the truth, to which He called you by our gospel, for the obtaining of the glory of our Lord Jesus Christ" (2 Thessalonians 2:13–14).

The beginning of God's gracious purposes carries us back before the beginning of the world. This choice was made in accordance with divine foreknowledge. This foreknowledge does not mean that God saw in advance or somehow predicted those who would come to believe in his Son and chose them on that basis. We know this because of such testimonies as that in Acts 13:48, where we read that Paul preached the gospel and "when the Gentiles heard this, they were glad and glorified the Word of the Lord. And as many as had been appointed to eternal life believed." The believing rests upon the appointing, rather than the appointing being a sort of predictive response to the believing. The appointment—the foreordination—came before and secured the believing that must surely follow.

It means that God's choice has its roots in eternity past and was made—in this particular sense—without reference to what his people would be, though it took full account of and made entire provision for our need as sinners.

Why Were They Chosen?

There are two strands in that question and its answer, and it is necessary that we address both.

On What Basis Were They Chosen?

<u>Not chosen out of merit.</u> Negatively, and as we have already begun to see in Acts 13:48, it was not because of any worthiness in us, either predicted or actual. The Lord has never dealt with people in this way. For example, in Deuteronomy 7:7 Moses assures Israel that "the LORD did not set His love on you nor choose you because you were more in number than any other people, for you were the least of all peoples." Israel at that time might have been tempted to look on the

multitudes of the tribes and say, "Ah, this is why God chose us. Look at how many of us there are! Truly we are just the kind of people whom God might have chosen for his glory!" We still face precisely the same kind of temptations—we imagine that our numbers, graces, abilities, faith, wealth, charisma, influence, or whatever else it might be, actually lies behind God's gift to us. In that scenario, salvation becomes a reward for what we already were or had become.

Scripturally, the truth is precisely the reverse. Indeed, we have to face the fact that "God has chosen the foolish things of the world to put to shame the wise, and God has chosen the weak things of the world to put to shame the things which are mighty" (1 Corinthians 1:27). In other words, if anything, God chose us not because of our exemplary giftedness or graciousness but because of our exemplary wretchedness and helplessness! Paul emphasizes that the cause of God's favorable dealings with us is not found in the working or the willing or the running (effort) of man:

> …(for the children not yet being born, nor having done any good or evil, that the purpose of God according to election might stand, not of works but of Him who calls), it was said to her, "The older shall serve the younger." As it is written, "Jacob I have loved, but Esau I have hated."…. So then it is not of him who wills, nor of him who runs, but of God who shows mercy. (Romans 9:11–13, 16)

Paul presses this home to the Corinthians when asking about the source of all the saving kindnesses that they enjoy: "For who makes you differ from another? And what do you have that you did not receive? Now if you did indeed receive it, why do you boast as if you had not received it?" (1 Corinthians 4:7).

Chosen out of mercy. Positively, in answering the same question, we see that this choice is rooted in the free mercy and sovereign love of Almighty God. It is an act of grace, utterly apart from or even in the face of the things that sinful mankind deserves, a gift freely given. So, while denying that God chose Israel because of any greatness in them, Moses traces the choice back to the heart of God:

> The LORD did not set His love on you nor choose you because you were more in number than any other people, for you were the least of all peoples; but because the LORD loves you, and because He would keep the oath which He swore to your fathers, the LORD has brought you out with a mighty hand, and redeemed you from the house of bondage, from the hand of Pharaoh king of Egypt. (Deuteronomy 7:7–8)

Writing to the Ephesian church, Paul sets their own native deadness against the new reality of life in Christ—that God, "even when we were dead in trespasses, made us alive together with Christ"—and then traces it to its divine source: "by grace you have been saved." Having so stated it in Ephesians 2:5, he repeats it again a few lines later for good measure: "For by grace you have been saved through faith, and that not of yourselves; it is the gift of God" (Ephesians 2:8).

Grace is God's free favor. It comes to the undeserving from outside them and apart from anything creditable in them (on the assumption that, apart from these mercies, any such thing could be discovered). It is, in this regard, entirely unconditional: it does not hinge or hang upon anything worthy that ever was, is, or will be in those who receive it.

To What End Were They Chosen?

But having asked on what basis God's elect are chosen, we must also ask *to what end were they chosen?* There are two elements to the answer.

For holiness. The first element is that they were chosen with a view to the holiness of men so saved. The election of God is so that we might stand before him in righteousness. It is true that we were saved to enjoy all the benefits of all the active and passive obedience of Christ—his provision of a perfect righteousness that is pleasing to God, and his suffering of all the punishment our sins deserve, so removing the curse from us. But it is also true that we were chosen and saved to be conformed to his image:

And we know that all things work together for

good to those who love God, to those who are the called according to His purpose. For whom He foreknew, He also predestined to be conformed to the image of His Son, that He might be the firstborn among many brethren. Moreover whom He predestined, these He also called; whom He called, these He also justified; and whom He justified, these He also glorified. (Romans 8:28–30)

Paul says as much to the Ephesians, emphasizing that God the Father "chose us in [Christ] before the foundation of the world, that we should be holy and without blame before Him in love" (Ephesians 1:4) and that "we are His workmanship, created in Christ Jesus for good works, which God prepared beforehand, that we should walk in them" (Ephesians 2:10). Good works do not feed into our election as an operating cause, but they do flow from it as an invariable consequence. Our Lord says, "You did not choose Me, but I chose you and appointed you that you should go and bear fruit, and that your fruit should remain, that whatever you ask the Father in My name He may give you" (John 15:16).

For God's glory. The second element of the answer to the question about the purpose of this election is the glory of God. Again, Paul hammers it home in the hymn of praise into which he invites the Ephesian church. All that the Lord does is "to the praise of the glory of His grace, by which He made us accepted in the Beloved" (Ephesians 1:6). God is working things according to the counsel of his will in order "that we who first trusted in Christ should be to the praise of His glory" (Ephesians 1:12). The grace of God is displayed to secure the praise of the glory of his grace. The ultimate intent of salvation is that God will be magnified by all those who enjoy and observe his lovingkindnesses, for Christians belong to "a chosen generation, a royal priesthood, a holy nation, His own special people, that you may proclaim the praises of Him who called you out of darkness into His marvelous light" (1 Peter 2:9).

God Behind Everything

What hangs behind all these gracious actions and trans-actions? It is the very being of God and his worthiness to be praised.

> Oh, the depth of the riches both of the wisdom and knowledge of God! How unsearchable are His judgments and His ways past finding out! "For who has known the mind of the LORD? Or who has become His counselor?" "Or who has first given to Him And it shall be repaid to him?" For of Him and through Him and to Him are all things, to whom be glory forever. Amen. (Romans 11:33–36)

Those who resent or deny these teachings must ask whether or not they have truly grasped something of the revealed glory of the unimaginably glorious God. Is such a person truly prepared to offer to the Lord of heaven and earth that which is his by virtue of who he is and by right of all that he does? We must let God be God!

Here we have, by all scriptural accounts and testimonies, an act of free, sovereign, gracious, merciful love. Given the heinous disposition and horrible condition of man as a sinful and sinning creature, all the initiative in salvation *must* come from God. All the saving good that man enjoys must arise from the Lord's deliberate and determinative love: "I will be gracious to whom I will be gracious, and I will have compassion on whom I will have compassion" (Exodus 33:19).

Who can deny that this is the prerogative of the holy and almighty and gracious One? It is the expression of his sovereignty considered in a general sense, a sovereignty well-attested by the Word of God:

> Then Job answered the LORD and said: "I know that You can do everything, And that no purpose of Yours can be withheld from You." (Job 42:1–2)

> But our God is in heaven; He does whatever He pleases. (Psalm 115:3)

> Whatever the LORD pleases He does, in heaven and in earth, in the seas and in all deep places. (Psalm 135:6)

Remember the former things of old, for I am God, and there is no other; I am God, and there is none like Me, declaring the end from the beginning, and from ancient times things that are not yet done, saying, "My counsel shall stand, and I will do all My pleasure," calling a bird of prey from the east, the man who executes My counsel, from a far country. Indeed I have spoken it; I will also bring it to pass. I have purposed it; I will also do it. (Isaiah 46:9–11)

In Him also we have obtained an inheritance, being predestined according to the purpose of Him who works all things according to the counsel of His will. (Ephesians 1:11)

More specifically, in his saving acts, the Lord is as much his own master as in everything else: "Salvation is of the LORD" (Jonah 2:9).

Our Proper Response

And so we ask, what can be and should be our response to such glorious truths as these? The Bible sends us in a number of delightful directions.

<u>Comfort</u>. Our first reaction might be *comfort*, because here is a reminder and an assurance that our salvation hangs upon God's sovereign choice and does not hinge upon our desperate desires and acts. If salvation depended upon my righteousness, my

strivings, my working, then I must be now condemned and forever damned. My life and happiness are secured, for time and for eternity, by a divine determination to save and to bless. There, and there only, can I find comfort in the midst of all trials and troubles.

Humility. There should also be *humility*, not only because of what we are by nature, in ourselves, but now also because we were chosen for blessing, not because of what we were but despite it. In ourselves, we are last and least of all:

> But God has chosen the foolish things of the world to put to shame the wise, and God has chosen the weak things of the world to put to shame the things which are mighty; and the base things of the world and the things which are despised God has chosen, and the things which are not, to bring to nothing the things that are, that no flesh should glory in His presence. (1 Corinthians 1:27–29)

We display God's grace because we are utterly undeserving. Our wretchedness is the stage on which God manifests his graciousness. Salvation never was something that we could claim in our own right, apart from Christ. Mercy is not something you can demand; you can only plead. More than that, we would never even have pleaded for it without being prompted and enabled. Here we lie in the dust, finding our proper place.

Confidence. Then again, there is *confidence*, because there is no such thing as a likely convert in this fallen world. There is only an election of grace. So we can freely proclaim the saving truth of God in the confident expectation that God's chosen people must come into his kingdom. He will give willing hearts to those who are in themselves unwilling. He will stir, awaken, and draw to himself all those upon whom he has set his love. Under divine influence, the most wretched, wrecked, reckless, and rotten rebels will come to Christ by God's appointment and be found among the chosen people of God. Ask Manasseh of Israel if it is so (2 Chronicles 33)! Ask Saul of Tarsus (Acts 9)!

Hope. It also promotes *hope*, for you and me and others. It means that when the gospel is proclaimed to someone outside the kingdom—when it came to us, if we are now Christians—then despite all that person is, has been, and has done, there is no reason why that one should not repent and believe. There is no reason pre-emptively to conclude that God has shut anyone out of his kingdom, no reason for the worst to despair of salvation. God saves sinners! The gospel offer is sincere and universal, and comes to all regardless of every other circumstance: "Come to Christ and be saved!"

Diligence. It requires of us *diligence*, that each one of us should make his calling and election sure (2 Peter 1:10). How will you resolve this matter in your own experience? Simply by believing and then obeying. The Scriptures never call an unconverted person to determine his election and then come to Christ. Rather, the call is to come to Christ and then go on in godliness. As the old illustration has it, salvation is a gate on which, as we approach it, we see written over it, "Whosoever shall call on the name of the LORD shall be saved." Passing through, we turn and see something more written on the inside, "Chosen from before the foundation of the world." If you would be saved, and be assured of it, then come to Christ. If you would have any be saved, urge them to call on the name of the Lord. Trust him and then, trusting, walk in his ways, and all the evidence we need of divine choosing and calling will be before us.

Praise. Finally, let there also be *praise*. If salvation is of the Lord, then the glory of salvation belongs to the Lord of salvation. All the initiative, the whole accomplishment, all comes from him. Our good is for his glory. Complain at that, if you will, as you look back at where you once were and where you would be still were it not for God's sovereign, saving choice. All we enjoy from his hand is intended to secure the praise of his glorious grace, and it is right and fitting that this should be so. No true saint would have it any other way. Great love is the only response to being so greatly loved. There is no hardship for a saved sinner in speaking of—singing of!—and serving for the glory of the God who saves.

Three
REDEEMED

How Is This Salvation Accomplished?

*I am the good shepherd. The good shepherd gives
His life for the sheep. But a hireling, he who is not
the shepherd, one who does not own the sheep,
sees the wolf coming and leaves the sheep and
flees; and the wolf catches the sheep and scatters
them. The hireling flees because he is a hireling
and does not care about the sheep. I am the good
shepherd; and I know My sheep, and am known
by My own. As the Father knows Me, even so I
know the Father; and I lay down My life for the
sheep. And other sheep I have which are not of
this fold; them also I must bring, and they will
hear My voice; and there will be one flock and
one shepherd. Therefore My Father loves Me,
because I lay down My life that I may take it
again. No one takes it from Me, but I lay it down
of Myself. I have power to lay it down, and I
have power to take it again. This command I
have received from My Father. (John 10:11–18)*

We need to consider our anchor points, the truths we must face and embrace if we are to be faithful to God in our doctrine and, consequently, in our practice. We began by asking, in effect, "Who needs to be saved?" Our answer was, every person. The answer takes account of the fallen condition of all mankind, and the answer is vital, because a false diagnosis will draw forth a false remedy, if one is considered necessary at all. Our next question was, "On what basis are sinners saved?" Our answer was, by virtue of being chosen by a sovereignly gracious God.

But those who are lost and chosen for salvation still need to *be* saved. And so we must now ask, "How is this salvation accomplished?" We need to consider by what means elect sinners are saved. How can we reconcile the three indisputable facts of a holy God, a lost world, and a saved church? Where do justice and mercy meet?

The answer to this question is simply this: God's chosen people are *redeemed*, they are purchased at a price. This is the third reality with which we must reckon. It points us to Christ's atoning death while also raising issues of the purpose and intent of that death, the design and result of the atonement. To begin addressing all this, we can start at John 10:11: "I am the good shepherd. The good shepherd gives His life for the sheep." Here we see the Redeemer, the redemption, and the redeemed.

The Redeemer: Our Good Shepherd

In these words Jesus of Nazareth describes himself as "the good shepherd." It is the Lord Christ who carries out this particular action in God's plan of redemption and he does so in this character. Here we are carried back to Paul's words to the Ephesian church:

> Grace to you and peace from God our Father and the Lord Jesus Christ. Blessed be the God and Father of our Lord Jesus Christ, who has blessed us with every spiritual blessing in the heavenly places in Christ, just as He chose us in Him before the foundation of the world, that we should be holy and without blame before Him in love, having predestined us to adoption as sons by Jesus Christ to Himself, according to the good pleasure of His will, to the praise of the glory of His grace, by which He made us accepted in the Beloved. (Ephesians 1:2–6)

We are blessed and chosen *in* Christ, in connection *with* him, associated *with* him from the beginning with respect to *all* of his saving acts and accomplishments.

Christ Jesus stands before us in John 10 as the incarnate God. It is vital that we grasp that truth and grip it firmly. In Matthew 1:21–23 the Lord is identified by two names which cannot be separated: Jesus and Immanuel. Mary's son will be called *Jesus*, for he will save his people from their sins. The virgin-born child shall be called by his name, *Immanuel*, which is translated, "God with us." He is Savior. He is God with us. If he is not the last he cannot be the first, for no blood and no righteousness but that of the God-man is sufficient for what is required. He is here as the Son of Man who came to seek and to save that which was lost (Luke 19:10; see also 15:4–7). Again, when we read that this good shepherd acted for or on behalf of others, we are carried immediately into the realm of substitution, of one taking the place of others. We are engaging with Isaiah's prophecy:

> Surely He has borne our griefs and carried our sorrows; yet we esteemed Him stricken, smitten by God, and afflicted. But He was wounded for our transgressions, He was bruised for our iniquities; the chastisement for our peace was upon Him, and by His stripes we are healed. All we like sheep have gone astray; we have turned, every one, to his own way; and the LORD has laid on Him the iniquity of us all.... He shall see the labor of His soul, and be satisfied. By His knowledge My righteous Servant shall justify many, for He shall bear their iniquities. (Isaiah 53:4–6, 11)

The Redemption: The Shepherd Gives His Life

What then did this Jesus-Immanuel, this good shepherd, do for others? The good shepherd laid down his life:

"Grace to you and peace from God the Father and our Lord Jesus Christ, *who gave Himself for our sins*, that He might deliver us from this present evil age, according to the will of our God and Father" (Galatians 1:3–4). He gave himself, shedding his blood, taking our punishment, paying our ransom, securing reconciliation: "And you, who once were alienated and enemies in your mind by wicked works, yet now He has reconciled in the body of His flesh through death, to present you holy, and blameless, and above reproach in His sight" (Colossians 1:21–22). This redemption secures all that is required by it and intended in it. In this act of redemption, Christ bears all the punishment the sin of his people deserves and secures all the glory to which God is entitled. All the enmity between God in his holiness and man in his sinfulness is removed, and all the blessing from a holy God for his needy people is obtained.

This redemption must be viewed in terms of its value and its efficacy.

Value of the Redemption

With regard to its *value*, we must not seek to measure the worth of the redemption by some formula or calculation, as if we could reckon up the extent of Christ's sufferings in proportion to God's saving intent. The value of the atonement hinges upon the excellence of the person who suffered. As the God-man, incarnate divinity, Christ's death was of infinite value in itself. It is simply beyond calculation. But this is precisely what the case requires. The sinfulness of our sin reflects and is revealed by the excellence of the person offended. The sinner's sin is against an infinitely holy God. Our sin is infinitely offensive for that reason, and so every condemned sinner needs an atonement of infinite value.

When we think of the effect of the atonement, especially in terms of its value, we often think and argue first in terms of its *extensive* range—how many people it affects. But perhaps that should not be our first concern. We need to consider its *intensive* requirements—how much sin it covers. We must take into account not only the question of those who are chosen but also the issue of how far they have fallen. When we speak of the value of Christ's atoning work, we should be considering and marveling at its quality before we begin to argue about its extent.

Efficacy of the Redemption

But then, with regard to its *efficacy*, we must grasp that the language used indicates not a possibility nor even a probability, but an actuality, a realized certainty. The grand result and definite purpose of Christ's death *was accomplished*. Paul tells us that "this is a faithful saying and worthy of all acceptance, that Christ Jesus came into the world to save sinners" (1 Timothy 1:15). Christ did not come to make sinners savable but actually to save them. He did not merely open a door for salvation, he carried his people through it. He laid down his life that sinners might live.

Of course, this does bring us to the question of the application of redemption. Christ died to save sinners... but how many and which ones?

The Redeemed: He Gives His Live for the Sheep

The Lord tells us that, as the good Shepherd, he lays down his life "for the sheep." There is *particularity* in this redemption. There is something definite in its intent and accomplishment. We are back to the question of God's purpose, design, and result.

If Christ died for *all the sins of all men*, then all must be saved. Clearly that is neither taught in the Scriptures nor seen in the world. If Christ died for *some sins of all men* then all are damned, and once again both revelation and experience forbid such a conclusion. We are left with only one other possibility: that Christ Jesus died for *all the sins of some people*. But who are they? He tells us: his sheep.

The same truth of a defined and purposeful saving intent is found throughout the Bible, revealed incidentally even when not stated explicitly. For example, Paul tells the married men in Ephesus to "love your wives, just as Christ also loved the church and gave Himself for her" (Ephesians 5:25). Woven into his instruction is the implicit assumption that Christ did not die for all men but for "the church," for whom specifically he gave himself. Or again, there is Peter's language to "the pilgrims of the Dispersion in Pontus, Galatia,

Cappadocia, Asia, and Bithynia, elect according to the foreknowledge of God the Father, in sanctification of the Spirit, for obedience and sprinkling of the blood of Jesus Christ" (1 Peter 1:1–2). These are the ones of pure faith, born of incorruptible seed, of whom it may be said that Christ "Himself bore our sins in His own body on the tree, that we, having died to sins, might live for righteousness — by whose stripes you were healed" (1 Peter 2:24). Again, there was a definite and directed intention in the sufferings and death of our Lord: he bore *our* sins.

Here the sweet logic of Scripture helps us, for we find and are assured that the extent of Christ's atoning work is identical with its divine intent. Its effect is entirely coordinate with the Father's choice: speaking of his sheep, the Lord says, "My Father…has given them to Me" (John 10:29). Salvation is accomplished in perfect accordance with God's design. The Son further expresses this confidence when he prays to the Father, recorded in John 17:

> Jesus spoke these words, lifted up His eyes to heaven, and said: "Father, the hour has come. Glorify Your Son, that Your Son also may glorify You, as You have given Him authority over all flesh, that He should give eternal life to as many as You have given Him. And this is eternal life, that they may know You, the only true God, and Jesus Christ whom You have sent. I have glorified You on the earth. I have finished the work which You have given Me

to do. And now, O Father, glorify Me together
with Yourself, with the glory which I had with You
before the world was. "I have manifested Your
name to the men whom You have given Me out
of the world. They were Yours, You gave them to
Me, and they have kept Your word. Now they have
known that all things which You have given Me
are from You. For I have given to them the words
which You have given Me; and they have received
them, and have known surely that I came forth from
You; and they have believed that You sent Me. "I
pray for them. I do not pray for the world but for
those whom You have given Me, for they are Yours.
And all Mine are Yours, and Yours are Mine, and
I am glorified in them. Now I am no longer in the
world, but these are in the world, and I come to You.
Holy Father, keep through Your name those whom
You have given Me, that they may be one as We
are.…I do not pray for these alone, but also for those
who will believe in Me through their word;…Father,
I desire that they also whom You gave Me may be
with Me where I am, that they may behold My glory
which You have given Me; for You loved Me before
the foundation of the world. O righteous Father!
The world has not known You, but I have known
You; and these have known that You sent Me. And
I have declared to them Your name, and will declare
it, that the love with which You loved Me may be in
them, and I in them." (John 17:1–11, 20, 24–26)

If Christ died for everyone, then he has failed spectacularly. If Christ died for no one in particular, then not only do we introduce a conflict into the Trinity (consider John 6:35–40) but we deny the Father his glory and the Son his reward.

But Christ died for *his* people, and he secured their salvation by his death. His church is elect from before time, is gathered together in time, and will be glorified with him at the end of time. That number cannot be added to or subtracted from: Christ has saved each and every one of his sheep by laying down his life for them.

Some will complain at this. "You are limiting the atonement! Where is the grace and the glory of God in that?" Well, every one of us limits the atonement, either in its breadth (its extent) or its depth (its effect). Christ's atonement is either universal (for all) or effectual (for some). It cannot be both, and there is neither grace nor glory in a salvation that does not save! Salvation is not limited in some narrow or shallow sense! It is definite! It is not for a scant few. It is for a great many! "For even the Son of Man did not come to be served, but to serve, and to give His life a ransom for *many*" (Mark 10:45; see also Matthew 20:28); "For this is My blood of the new covenant, which is shed for *many* for the remission of sins" (Matthew 26:28); "Christ was offered once to bear the sins of *many*" (Hebrews 9:28).

How many? Countless! Christ's redeemed ones are a multitude beyond numbering, gathered in from every part of his world: "After these things I looked, and behold, a great multitude which no one could number, of all nations, tribes, peoples, and tongues, standing before the throne and before the Lamb, clothed with white robes, with palm branches in their hands" (Revelation 7:9).

Men and women are all, by nature, dead in their trespasses and sins. All would remain so, utterly and entirely lost, unless God in sovereign mercy chose some for salvation. Having chosen them, God has in Christ redeemed them, securing a complete salvation for every single one of his people. Not one of all his elect has been excluded, overlooked, or unaccounted for.

Let us wonder. This is a matter of *wonder*, that the love of God should extend to this. Who would have dared dream that sinners should be redeemed by the death of God's only Son? "When we were enemies we were reconciled to God through the death of His Son" (Romans 5:10). It is the very demonstration and definition of love: "In this the love of God was manifested toward us, that God has sent His only begotten Son into the world, that we might live through Him. In this is love, not that we loved God, but that He loved us and sent His Son to be the propitiation for our sins" (1 John 4:9–10).

Redemption could be accomplished at no lower price. This was its inescapable cost, and divine love paid the price.

Let us praise. But it is also a cause for *praise* because it is accomplished. God has done it! There is nothing lacking in it. He has done it in a way that honors his justice and exalts his mercy. Salvation is secured in a way that both displays his grace and secures his glory. All the divine perfections are most magnified in this great work. If you would know God, you will see him shining most clearly and most brightly in the gloom of Golgotha.

Let us give thanks. It is a reason for *thanksgiving*. It was provided for sinners. We are the recipients of this mercy. If you are a Christian, you are the beneficiary of God's saving intention and labor. It is now being applied to you in all its saving fullness. It belongs to you in its entirety and all its phases and expressions, past, present, and future, earthly and heavenly, temporally and eternally. All that is included in it is yours, and must be yours, and cannot fail to be yours, and time would fail us to tell out the wonders of redeeming grace stored up for the saints in Christ Jesus!

Let us be confident. It gives us great *confidence* because all is settled. Nothing is lacking in our salvation, either in the quality of the redemption or the extent of its application by divine design. Christ's death saves his people perfectly, entirely, utterly, and surely. Nothing needs to be made up, for nothing is lacking. No one needs to add to it, and no one and nothing can damage, destroy, or defeat it.

Let us serve. It moves us to *service*. "Or do you not know that your body is the temple of the Holy Spirit who is in you, whom you have from God, and you are not your own? For you were bought at a price;

therefore glorify God in your body and in your spirit, which are God's" (1 Corinthians 6:19–20). We no longer belong to ourselves, but the life we now live we live to him who loved us and gave his life for us. That act of sacrifice revealed a love "so amazing, so divine" that it "demands my soul, my life, my all."[4] It robs us of all excuses and strips us of all carelessness. It makes us ask,

> How can I, Lord, withhold life's brightest hour
> From Thee, or gathered gold, or any power?
> Why should I keep one precious thing from Thee
> When Thou hast given Thine own dear self for me?[5]

If the love of God in Christ does not capture and enrapture our hearts then we should dwell upon it humbly and prayerfully until it begins to move us.

Let us witness. It imposes on the saints a measure of *responsibility*. We have the privilege of declaring the good news of salvation in Christ Jesus our Lord, calling sinners to repent of their sins and to believe in him. On any other basis than the finished and definite work of Christ, the preaching of the gospel is a fool's errand. This is true whether or not we acknowledge it to be so! With this reality to rest on, we have an answer to the question, "What must I do to be saved?" (Acts 16:31). If Christ died for all, there would be no point in preaching; if Christ's death were ineffective, there would be no point in offering salvation; if Christ died for no one in particular, we have no prospect of success. But if Christ died to save *his people* from their sins, if the Shepherd laid down his life to secure the life of *his sheep*, then we have a reason to go to sinners, and something to say when we reach them!

Let us be encouraged. Finally, it affords to every broken heart sweet *encouragement*. Sinners like us can come to a perfect Savior to obtain a complete and effectual salvation. If you go to Christ, he will not turn you away: "All that the Father gives Me will come to Me, and the one who comes to Me I will by no means cast out" (John 6:37). Christ assures us in the strongest terms that "this is the will of Him who sent Me, that everyone who sees the Son and believes in Him may have everlasting life; and I will raise him up at the last day" (John 6:40; see also v 47). Everything that the penitent sinner needs is in Christ Jesus. Whoever turns to him in faith will be delivered from sin, with all its guilt and punishment and power, saved with God's so-great salvation, redeemed by the blood of the Lamb of God.

Four

CALLED

How Do We Come to Possess the Blessings of Salvation?

And we know that all things work together for good to those who love God, to those who are the called according to His purpose. For whom He foreknew, He also predestined to be conformed to the image of His Son, that He might be the firstborn among many brethren. Moreover whom He predestined, these He also called; whom He called, these He also justified; and whom He justified, these He also glorified. (Romans 8:28–30)

We have so far considered three anchor points of the Bible's teaching about the grace of God, truths to which we must hold fast in the present generation and pass on to coming generations. In the preceding pages we have seen that we are by nature *fallen*, facing our rebellion and our utter spiritual deadness and hopelessness in ourselves as lost sinners. Then we saw that

Christians are *chosen*, the Lord God — in the face of our hell-deserving sinfulness — freely and sovereignly setting his love upon us, saving whom he will. Next, we traced how we are *redeemed*, the Lord Christ Jesus laying down his life to save all those whom the Father had given him.

All this carries us on to another question: if there are those in utter lostness and misery who are appointed for mercy, and if this blessing of life has been secured for them, their ransom paid by Christ, how does anyone enter into possession of those blessings?

The answer to the question is we must be *called*. Here is another anchor point for faith.

The Necessity of the Call

The fact that this call is necessary flows from and is demanded by all that has gone before. By nature we can neither understand nor receive those things which belong to the Spirit of God — they are foolishness to the natural man, nor can he know them, because they are spiritually discerned (1 Corinthians 2:14). We are spiritually lifeless, antagonistic to righteousness, slaves of sin, blind and deaf to divine truth, having no capacity either to know or to do the will of God, sinful in nature and by deed. As should be plain from all that we have considered before, unless God works to save us, we simply cannot be saved. Unless God calls us to himself, we cannot but remain where we are — wandering, inert, rebelling. Think of the composite picture of hopelessness and helplessness in the parable of Luke 15 — a lost sheep, a lost coin, a lost son. This is the heart of every man by nature. But the merciful promise of God takes account of this. In Ezekiel 36 the Lord promises a new heart and spirit, moving us to will and to do in accordance with the Word of God:

> I will give you a new heart and put a new spirit within you; I will take the heart of stone out of your flesh and give you a heart of flesh. I will put My Spirit within you and cause you to walk in My statutes, and you will keep My judgments and do them. (Ezekiel 36:26–27)

Similarly pressing language is found in John's Gospel. Speaking to Nicodemus, Jesus says to him, "Most assuredly, I say to you, unless one is born again, he cannot see the kingdom of God" (John 3:3), before driving home the fact: "Do not marvel that I said to you, 'You must be born again'" (John 3:7). Christ is not telling Nicodemus about an obligation to fulfill, but about a necessary experience to undergo. Nicodemus — like all of us — must be born again if he is to enter the kingdom of heaven. Unless God calls us to himself, we shall remain lost in the darkness, stuck just where we are.

The Nature of the Call

Here we must make a distinction between two different kinds of call that come from God.

The Universal Call

There is, first of all, *the general or universal gospel invitation*. It is variously described and depicted in the Old Testament and in the New:

"Ho! Everyone who thirsts, come to the waters; and you who have no money, come, buy and eat. Yes, come, buy wine and milk without money and without price. Why do you spend money for what is not bread, and your wages for what does not satisfy? Listen carefully to Me, and eat what is good, and let your soul delight itself in abundance. Incline your ear, and come to Me. Hear, and your soul shall live; and I will make an everlasting covenant with you—the sure mercies of David. Indeed I have given him as a witness to the people, a leader and commander for the people. Surely you shall call a nation you do not know, and nations who do not know you shall run to you, Because of the LORD your God, and the Holy One of Israel; For He has glorified you." Seek the LORD while He may be found, call upon Him while He is near. Let the wicked forsake his way, and the unrighteous man his thoughts; let him return to the LORD, and He will have mercy on him; and to our God, for He will abundantly pardon. (Isaiah 55:1–7)

Thus says the LORD: "Stand in the ways and see, and ask for the old paths, where the good way is, and walk in it; then you will find rest for your souls. But they said, 'We will not walk in it.'" (Jeremiah 6:16)

Jesus answered and said to them, "This is the work of God, that you believe in Him whom He sent." (John 6:29)

"While you have the light, believe in the light, that you may become sons of light." These things Jesus spoke, and departed, and was hidden from them. (John 12:36)

These are just a few brief and scattered examples of a Bible full of admonitions, pleas, and commands to hear God's Word, receive God's Christ, take God's promises, flee God's wrath. Sinners are repeatedly urged to repent of sin and believe in the Lord Christ. This gospel call comes to all, urging all to come to Christ and so to obtain life everlasting. In accordance with this, it is the task of preachers to declare the good news, identifying and exposing sin and making plain the context, substance, and demands of the gospel of God. Preachers, on behalf of God, are to call, command, persuade, and entreat sinners to be reconciled to God. But although that general invitation should be made, and is made on God's terms by faithful gospel ministers, mankind is by nature unwilling to come (Matthew 22:3, 23:37; John 5:40). Something more is required.

The Effectual Call

And so we come, second, to *the effectual gospel call*.
This is not separate from the general gospel invitation.
It both lies within it and rides above it. The Shorter
Catechism (Question 32) defines this effectual call with
beautiful, biblical precision and clarity:

> Effectual calling is the work of God the Father's
> power and grace, whereby He, by His Word
> and Spirit, invites and draws His elect unto Jesus
> Christ; convincing them of their sin and misery,
> enlightening their minds in the knowledge of
> Christ, and renewing their wills, thereby persuad-
> ing and enabling them to embrace Jesus Christ,
> freely offered to all in the gospel.[6]

This call, then, is more than a gracious and genuine
invitation. It is a sovereign summons. This powerful
call actually accomplishes something. It secures its
intended outcome. It is something like the difference
between a birthday invitation and a court summons.
The first can be fairly easily turned down with little
thought and little consequence. The other comes with
an authority that cannot be denied. For this reason Paul
can write that while one sows and another waters, it is
God who gives the increase (1 Corinthians 3:6–7). He
calls in accordance with his own gracious purposes in
Christ:

And we know that all things work together for good to those who love God, to those who are the called according to His purpose. For whom He foreknew, He also predestined to be conformed to the image of His Son, that He might be the firstborn among many brethren. Moreover whom He predestined, these He also called; whom He called, these He also justified; and whom He justified, these He also glorified" (Romans 8:28–30).

All those who are chosen and redeemed shall, in due course, be called. But *why* is this call effectual?

The Power of the Call

The reason for the power of the call lies in its author and its agent. As the Word of God is preached or read or discussed, the call comes from God the Father by God the Holy Spirit. In the declaration of the good news, the Holy Spirit comes into personal and purposeful contact with the dead soul of a sinner and he — who previously could neither know nor discern spiritual things — begins to see things accurately, feel things truly, and respond accordingly.

This is a divine act, a sovereign act: "Of His own will He brought us forth by the word of truth, that we might be a kind of firstfruits of His creatures" (James 1:18). It does not in any way depend for success on the man who is being called, anything he is, or anything that is in him. The one being effectually called is a dead man being made alive. He is not operating at this point but being operated upon. The Word of God comes, but it comes now in power, and in the Holy Spirit, and in much assurance (1 Thessalonians 1:5). It accomplishes God's purpose.

The Effect of the Call

Listen to the words of our Lord:

> "All that the Father gives Me will come to Me, and the one who comes to Me I will by no means cast out....No one can come to Me unless the Father who sent Me draws him; and I will raise him up at the last day. It is written in the prophets, 'And they shall all be taught by God.' Therefore everyone who has heard and learned from the Father comes to Me....But there are some of you who do not believe." For Jesus knew from the beginning who they were who did not believe, and who would betray Him. And He said, "Therefore I have said to you that no one can come to Me unless it has been granted to him by My Father." (John 6:37, 44–45, 64–65)

Here is the effect of the Spirit's work. Sometimes we speak of irresistible grace, but that might be taken to suggest that the rebellious sinner keeps resisting and is brought to Christ against his will. But what do we have in these words of the Lord Jesus? Not the demonstration of violent force so that a man is moved contrary to his will, as if we are saved kicking and screaming against it. Neither do we find the suspension of a man's faculties so that he becomes a puppet or a robot. Rather, under the gracious influence of the Holy Spirit, his rebellious heart is subdued and he is made willing and so comes willingly to Christ. He is brought from darkness to light by this powerful, effectual call (1 Peter 2:9): "He has delivered us from the power of darkness and conveyed us into the kingdom of the Son of His love" (Colossians 1:13). He is carried from death to life by the potent operations of the Spirit of Christ, and seeing both himself and his Savior clearly for the first time, the sinner casts himself on the Ransomer with repentance and in faith and so finds peace with God as a justified sinner (Romans 8:30).

But a further question arises: What does this look like and feel like in the life of the sinner?

The Experience of the Call

There is a real danger here. There are some extremely well-known spiritual life stories, biographies, and autobiographies that trace, sometimes in great and even excruciating detail, the course by which a sinner was finally brought humbly to the Savior. The danger is that, in reading these histories, a sensitive soul might begin to impose that pattern on his or her own life, expecting or even demanding to see precisely the same trajectory mapped out in their own experience. What should be considered merely descriptive becomes unreasonably prescriptive. Much harm can be done by making such histories an absolute standard by which legitimate and genuine spiritual experience must be assessed. Such an approach can leave some genuine seekers suspended in gloom, believing that they cannot come to God without undergoing a particular experience, either in kind or degree. In the same way, some true believers may be left without assurance because they are still looking for something the Lord neither demanded nor promised.

There Is Uniformity

So we must see that there is *a measure of uniformity* in our experience. Certain things will be and must be part of this experience for all the saints. There will usually be a measure of conviction of sin, and of righteousness, and of judgment (John 16.8). As the Word of God is read and explained and applied, the sinner will come to recognize the accuracy of the divine diagnosis concerning the fallen heart with the excellency of the divine provision for the sinful soul. There may be reasons raised or excuses offered why that sinner is or should be kept from the Lamb of God, but these will be gradually or suddenly addressed or removed. Then, with a willing heart, the sinner—now enlivened by the Holy Spirit—will put his faith in the Lord Jesus Christ, turning from sin to him, and so be delivered from death and hell, and enter into—usually with increasing awareness and vigor—the blessing of God's redemption and the joy of salvation.

There Is Variety

Then we must further recognize that there is *a measure of variety* in our experience, and that this is not only legitimate but appropriate, even to the point of being exquisite. Certain elements will always be present and a certain sequence will never be disordered (for example, repentance and faith will always follow the act of the Holy Spirit by which a heart is made new). However, there may be different timescales involving different degrees of intensity. Some may spend months or even years under conviction of sin, some only minutes or even moments. Some may feel carried to the very gates of hell by their guilt, others may be less deeply, though no less sincerely, troubled. Some may come gradually to feel their need of a Savior, their hearts opened to heed the truth of God, like Lydia (Acts 16:14); some may be shaken violently into an awareness of their condition, coming to Christ in a righteous panic, like the Philippian jailer (Acts 16:29–31). Some may be very young and tender, gently moved by the Holy Spirit and barely aware of the transition from death to life; others may be older or harder, subject to more apparently vigorous operations of the Spirit of God. Some may be converted the first time the gospel comes to their ears; some may not be saved until they have heard five thousand sermons. But all who are saved have heard the call of God in the gospel and, under the influence of the Holy Spirit, have come to Christ for life, repenting and believing.

Because of the Call

<u>Certainty.</u> For believers in Christ all of this should give rise, first and foremost, to *certainty* — the certainty that every one of God's chosen people shall be brought into his kingdom. The Holy Spirit never fails to bring to salvation those sinners whom he personally calls to Jesus. The redemption that has been accomplished through the atoning blood of our Savior, the Lord Jesus, shall be definitely and effectively applied to all for whom it was accomplished.

<u>Prayer.</u> Furthermore, and on that basis, it should give rise to *prayer* for the Holy Spirit to work in the hearts of those who hear the gospel. The fact that God *will* save does not for one moment preclude earnest and believing prayer for the Lord *to* save. We must pray that the Spirit would convince sinners of their sin and misery, enlighten their minds in the knowledge of Christ, and renew their wills, thereby persuading and enabling them to embrace Christ Jesus, freely offered to all men in the gospel. Do we sufficiently believe in the power and the grace of God to make this a more constant and more earnest plea?

<u>Proclamation.</u> It should also promote *proclamation*. We must make the gospel known. In the Scriptures, people trust in Jesus after they hear the word of truth, the gospel of salvation (Ephesians 1:13). "Faith comes by hearing, and hearing by the word of God" (Romans 10:17), which is why Paul asks,

How then shall they call on Him in whom they
have not believed? And how shall they believe
in Him of whom they have not heard? And how
shall they hear without a preacher? And how shall
they preach unless they are sent? As it is written:
"How beautiful are the feet of those who preach
the gospel of peace, who bring glad tidings of good
things!" (Romans 10:14–15).

We must send forth the universal gospel invitation,
preaching without restraint or doubt, indiscriminately
"gospelling" a fallen world. The church is called to
declare a crucified Christ. Our privilege is to proclaim
the praises of him who called us out of darkness into
his marvelous light (1 Peter 2:9). The Holy Spirit uses
means, and the primary means is the clear and unadul-
terated proclamation of the gospel of Christ.

Confidence. All this provides strong *confidence*,
because the fruit of our labors as witnesses to Christ
does not at all depend on the devil's malign will.
Neither does it hang upon the fallen and perverted
will of the men to whom we preach. It depends on the
gracious will of a saving God, who has set his sovereign
love upon a people, redeemed them, and is now—in
time and space, one by one, sometimes singly and
sometimes several at once, here and there—calling that
people to himself.

Praise. And so this should certainly give rise to
praise. The more we study this, I trust we are the more

persuaded that salvation is of the Lord. It has its origins in his sovereign love and free grace. It is — considered as a whole and in all its parts — a gift bestowed on the utterly undeserving, to the glory of God the Giver.

Assessment. All this also calls us to make a careful *assessment*. Believers are told to make their calling and election sure (2 Peter 1:10). In doing this, we must be careful to ask the right questions. The starting point and foundation is this: *have you, hearing the gospel, accepted God's diagnosis of your sinful state, and so come to Christ Jesus as God's remedy for your condition, repenting of your sin and trusting in Christ?* If you have come in this way, it is because the Lord God has called you and drawn you to himself. It is the only explanation for these mercies. Faith only grows in the soil of a renewed heart.

Action. Finally, I hope, if necessary, that there may be some readers whom it will prompt to *action*. Perhaps you have read these things, but have you grasped them? You have perhaps listened to preachers or other friends tell you the good news of salvation, but have you ever really heard? Have you done more than simply register the facts of the gospel? Have you felt the force of truth? If you have, will you turn now from sin to Christ, trusting in him, and so have life?

Five
ENDURING

How Do We Remain in Christ to the End?

*Blessed be the God and Father of our Lord Jesus
Christ, who according to His abundant mercy
has begotten us again to a living hope through
the resurrection of Jesus Christ from the dead, to
an inheritance incorruptible and undefiled and
that does not fade away, reserved in heaven for
you, who are kept by the power of God through
faith for salvation ready to be revealed in the last
time. (1 Peter 1:3–5)*

Neither Christ nor any of his faithful followers
ever described the Christian life as a stroll in the park. It
always was and always will be a battle to the end. When
Paul and Barnabas strengthened the souls of the disciples
in various places, they urged them to continue in the
faith, saying, "We must through many tribulations enter
the kingdom of God" (Acts 14:22). This is the experience of true saints. There are struggles within and storms
without. There may be times when we wonder, "Shall

I stand? Will I at last enter the heavenly kingdom?" In terms of the brief studies in this book, we have been tracing some of the prominent anchor points of the Christian faith. From the pages of God's book we have seen that Christians are fallen, chosen, redeemed, and called. But, having fallen once in Adam and having been lost, can we fall again and be lost again? Having stumbled so often ourselves, might we so stumble as to fall away entirely and be damned at last? One old preacher called William O'Neill put the question in this way: "Is it possible for sincere Christians, truly regenerated persons, to be finally separated from Jesus, to lose the favor of God their Father, and be eternally shut out from his smile and home?"[7] That is a massive question. Its answer is of enormous weight and eternal significance.

The Bible gives us the answer. Christians are by nature fallen, by grace chosen, redeemed, and called. As a consequence of this display of grace, they shall also be enduring. In studying this aspect of God's grace toward sinners, we should notice two subtle but definite shifts: a shift from the past tense to the present, looking toward the future; and a shift from a more passive sense and voice toward a more active notion. This reflects the two sides of the coin of a Christian's safe and sure enduring, both being found throughout Scripture.

The Preservation of the Saints

Our emphasis throughout these studies in God's grace has been that salvation is of the Lord. That is equally true here. The God who chose his people, who redeemed us and called us, will keep us to the end. This lies behind and beneath any notion of the saints' perseverance to the end. The Bible is awash with testimonies to God's preserving grace. We will identify and arrange just a few.

Embrace God's Purposes

We can think in terms of the *purposes of God*. "The gifts and the calling of God are irrevocable" (Romans 11:29)—they will not be called back or revoked, and they shall not fail. As you trawl through the Old Testament it is clear that the Lord intends to call and then to *keep* a people. There may be nuances to these assurances, as we work from national Israel forward to the new covenant people of God, comprising both Jews and Gentiles, but that should not make us undermine or dismiss these things. Often the principle abides even when the application changes. So, for example, we find Samuel promising that "the LORD will not forsake His people, for His great name's sake, because it has pleased the LORD to make you His people" (1 Samuel 12:22). Through Isaiah he reminds them that there are variations in their experience, but no shifts in the enduring purposes of God: "'For a mere moment I have forsaken you, but with great mercies I will gather you. With a little wrath I hid My face from you for a moment; but with everlasting kindness I will have mercy on you,' Says the LORD, your Redeemer" (Isaiah 54:7–8).

Jeremiah offers this assurance: "The LORD has appeared of old to me, saying: "Yes, I have loved you with an everlasting love; therefore with lovingkindness I have drawn you" (Jeremiah 31:3). Grounded in these things, the same prophet goes on to define the new covenant in absolute terms:

> Behold, the days are coming, says the LORD, when I will make a new covenant with the house of Israel and with the house of Judah—not according to the covenant that I made with their fathers in the day that I took them by the hand to lead them out of the land of Egypt, My covenant which they broke, though I was a husband to them, says the LORD. But this is the covenant that I will make with the house of Israel after those days, says the LORD: I will put My law in their minds, and write it on their hearts; and I will be their God, and they shall be My people. No more shall every man teach his neighbor, and every man his brother, saying, "Know the LORD," for they all shall know Me, from the least of them to the greatest of them, says the LORD. For I will forgive their iniquity, and their sin I will remember no more. (Jeremiah 31:31–34)

The same note of certainty rings throughout the New Testament. It is there in the declaration of our Lord Jesus that "this is the will of the Father who sent Me, that of all He has given Me I should lose nothing, but should raise it up at the last day" (John 6:39). It is plainly implied in Paul's confidence regarding the church in Thessalonica: "But we are bound to give thanks to God always for you, brethren beloved by the Lord, because God from the beginning chose you for salvation through sanctification by the Spirit and belief in the truth" (2 Thessalonians 2:13). God chose them from the beginning for salvation, which—in the context—is not merely a thing that lies in the past, but a reality that buoys them in the present and stretches surely into the future. Peter, too, can assure the saints to whom he writes that they have "been born again, not of corruptible seed but incorruptible, through the word of God which lives and abides forever" (1 Peter 1:23).

Or we might note the holy and unshakable logic of Romans 8:30: "Moreover whom He predestined, these He also called; whom He called, these He also justified; and whom He justified, these He also glorified." This golden chain of divine purpose carries every chosen child of God safely and securely into glory itself.

Rest on God's Promises

Next, we should consider the *promises of God*, stated and implied. Again, we are faced with an embarrassment of riches. Provided with an enormous tray of chocolates, we select just a few.

Notice first the way the Lord Jesus speaks in John 5:24, beginning with the formula of guarantee. Here we have not just a matter of absolute conviction but of absolute certainty: "*Most assuredly*, I say to you, he who hears My word and believes in Him who sent Me *has* everlasting life, and *shall not* come into judgment, but *has* passed from death into life" (John 5:24). The same sort of pledge is offered again: "Most assuredly, I say to you, he who believes in Me *has* everlasting life" (John 6:47).

Not long afterward, speaking of those who believe in him, he says, "This is the bread which comes down from heaven, that one may eat of it and not die. I am the living bread which came down from heaven. If anyone eats of this bread, he will live forever; and the bread that I shall give is My flesh, which I shall give for the life of the world" (John 6:50–51). He goes on to make this solemn declaration, that "as the living Father sent Me, and I live because of the Father, so he who feeds on Me will live because of Me" (John 6:57).

In similar fashion, the apostle Paul can speak to the church in Philippi and tell them without a tremor that he is "confident of this very thing, that He who has begun a good work in you will complete it until the day of Jesus Christ" (Philippians 1:6). He makes plain to the Colossians in similar language to that found in other letters, that each of them should "set your mind on things above, not on things on the earth. For you died, and your life is hidden with Christ in God. When Christ who is our life appears, then you also will appear with Him in glory" (Colossians 3:2–4). Finally, there is the stirring string of negatives of Hebrews 13:5: "Let your conduct be without covetousness; be content with such things as you have. For He Himself has said, 'I will never leave you nor forsake you.'"

Reading through such words as these, can we doubt that God has saved and is saving and will save his redeemed people?

Accept God's Providences

Move on with me to the *providences of God*. The divine government of the entire world is conducted with the end in view of the final salvation of the people of God. So Joseph can assure his brothers, giving us a window into the wise and sure designs of the Lord, that even the things that they meant for evil, God intended for good (Genesis 50:20). The same kind of assurance is offered on the broadest scale by the apostle Paul when writing to the church in Rome: "And we know that all things work together for good to those who love God, to those who are the called according to His purpose. For whom He foreknew, He also predestined to be conformed to the image of His Son, that He might be the firstborn among many brethren" (Romans 8:28–29). When God calls for the purpose of conforming to the image of his Son, Jesus Christ—not just a gradual increase in likeness, but working toward a final and complete transformation—then he orders all things to work together for that good and holy and sure purpose.

God will work out all his purposes, including those for his redeemed people, even though his providences may seem to run counter to his promises. As surely as Joseph would be elevated above the brothers who threw him in a pit and sold him as a slave, so surely the worst that any child of God experiences is a means in the hands of his heavenly Father to conform him now to the image of Christ and to move him inexorably toward the glory that lies ahead. We must not forget that some of these things fall very firmly into the category of fatherly chastening. The writer to the Hebrews compares God the Father's loving treatment of his adopted children with the behavior of a godly and gracious earthly father: "For they indeed for a few days chastened us as seemed best to them, but He for our profit, that we may be partakers of His holiness. Now no chastening seems to be joyful for the present, but painful; nevertheless, afterward it yields the peaceable fruit of righteousness to those who have been trained by it" (Hebrews 12:10–11; see also Isaiah 54:7–8). Sometimes those experiences that are most painful are most profitable in God's plan for our sanctification—our increasing holiness—so that we learn to say, "It is good for me that I have been afflicted, that I may learn Your statutes" (Psalm 119:71).

Rejoice in God's Provisions

Think also of the *provisions of God*. These might be thought of as a subset of his providences, but they are worthy of consideration in their own right. This is the purposeful and deliberate giving of all that is needful for the standing fast and holding to the end of every one of God's children. He has provided everything we require. At its most basic, the gift of God's son has secured everlasting life: "For God so loved the world that He gave His only begotten Son, that whoever believes in Him should not perish but have everlasting life" (John 3:16). Not only his atoning death but his abiding life ensure that we shall be saved: "For if when we were enemies we were reconciled to God through the death of His Son, much more, having been reconciled, we shall be saved by His life" (Romans 5:10).

Paul can therefore hit us with a barrage of questions designed to strip away all fears and remove all doubts:

> What then shall we say to these things? If God is for us, who can be against us? He who did not spare His own Son, but delivered Him up for us all, how shall He not with Him also freely give us all things? Who shall bring a charge against God's elect? It is God who justifies. Who is he who condemns? It is Christ who died, and furthermore is also risen, who is even at the right hand of God, who also makes intercession for us. (Romans 8:31–34)

Perhaps the sweetest assurance of all is that Christ himself is with us. Before he ascended into heaven he spoke to his disciples, issuing commands and offering comforts:

All authority has been given to Me in heaven and on earth. Go therefore and make disciples of all the nations, baptizing them in the name of the Father and of the Son and of the Holy Spirit, teaching them to observe all things that I have commanded you; and lo, I am with you always, even to the end of the age. Amen. (Matthew 28:18–20)

This promise of his ongoing presence he fulfils in various ways, primarily through the presence of his Holy Spirit in the heart of every saint and in the church at large, though we should not forget his intercessory prayers on our behalf (Hebrews 7:25). But he also, as the Good Shepherd of the sheep, supplies needful things in the church as a means of caring for his flock, taking account of all the challenges and demands of kingdom life in a fallen world:

And He Himself gave some to be apostles, some prophets, some evangelists, and some pastors and teachers, for the equipping of the saints for the work of ministry, for the edifying of the body of Christ, till we all come to the unity of the faith and of the knowledge of the Son of God, to a perfect man, to the measure of the stature of the fullness of Christ; that we should no longer be children, tossed to and fro and carried about with every wind of doctrine, by the trickery of men, in the cunning craftiness of deceitful plotting, but, speaking the truth in love,

may grow up in all things into Him who is the
head—Christ—from whom the whole body, joined
and knit together by what every joint supplies,
according to the effective working by which every
part does its share, causes growth of the body for
the edifying of itself in love. (Ephesians 4:11–16)

Alongside of such ministers and their various
labors in speaking the truth, Christ has provided other
means of grace and avenues of blessing. These include
baptism and the Lord's supper, prayer and song, with
various aspects of the fellowship of the saints in the
embrace of his church. The Lord gives all these to
promote the well-being of his people and to strengthen
and to nurture the spiritual life granted to them. While
there are individual battles to fight, and a personal
journey to make, it is with and among the people of
God that the pilgrim's progress takes place.

We should never lose sight of the corporate
dimension of this journey. We stand and we fight and
we go both individually and collectively, members
together of the one body. Our fellow travellers, and
our various supplies along the way, are all part of God's
provision for us. In Christ and from Christ we find all
that is necessary for all the people of Christ to stand fast.

Obey God's Precepts

Furthermore, we must take into account the *precepts
of God*. It would be far too easy to remove these from

the equation, but to do so would not only be foolish but potentially fatal. Signs indicating the right path and warnings to stay away from the cliff edge keep the traveler from falling to his death. In the same way, God tells us how to live in order that we might keep on the way of life.

He sends to us teachers in order to instruct us how to live in safety and security, communicating his truth: "Your ears shall hear a word behind you, saying, 'This is the way, walk in it,' whenever you turn to the right hand or whenever you turn to the left" (Isaiah 30:21). These teachers warn and teach in all wisdom in order that they might present every man perfect in Christ Jesus (Colossians 1:28). He commands us to make our calling and election sure (1 Peter 1:10) and equips us to do so. Noticeably, most of the assurances and commitments to which we have referred above come to us in immediate connection with calls to obedience (see, for example, Ephesians 6:10–13; Colossians 3:5, 12; 2 Thessalonians 2:13–15; or Hebrews 10:12, 23–26). God's promises and provisions should never be isolated from his precepts.

Trust in God Himself

Our confidence and our comfort are rooted in the determinate purpose and saving activity of God Almighty. We cannot escape the personal nature of this, nor that all three persons of the Godhead are actively and intimately involved in this work. This is a salvation of trinitarian scope and power. It is God's will that all those given to the Son should be kept to and through the last day (John 6:39). The eternal life of the saints is the life of those who are held in the hand of the Son and of the Father, who are one (John 10:28–30). God does not forget us; in the person of the incarnate Son, our names are inscribed on the palms of his hands (Isaiah 49:15–16). The Lord Jesus prays for his people that their faith should not fail in the face of particular trials and temptations, and he does so for each one as required (Luke 22:31–32, Hebrews 7:25). By the Holy Spirit, who is the guarantee of our inheritance until the redemption of the purchased possession, the children of God are sealed until that day of redemption (Ephesians 1:13–14, 4:30). We are held in the grip of the Almighty, kept by the power of God through faith for salvation ready to be revealed in the last time (1 Peter 1:5).

The Perseverance of the Saints

The apostle Peter's words in 1 Peter 1:5 carry us to a corresponding truth that we must consider, for we are kept by the power of God through faith. The certainty and security of God's people should never breed passivity or carelessness in true saints. Again, listen to William O'Neill's sweet but searching words: "that doctrine [of the security of the saints] was never designed to comfort any man who is not living a life of faith in the Son of God, intensely anxious to please God in all things — to be the holy and happy subject of that mind which was in Christ Jesus."[8]

You might sometimes hear the formula, "Once saved, always saved." Those phrases so linked are true insofar as they go, but some interpret them as jumping from the distant past to the distant future without any reference to the immediate present. So many imagine that they are saved because they once prayed a sinner's prayer, walked an aisle at the invitation of a preacher, raised their hand when Christ was offered, made a decision for Jesus, or something of that order. However, many who have done those things at some point, perhaps more than once in some cases, then live without any reference to God, without any regard for the means of grace, without any thought of abiding and increasing holiness. They seem to be deluded into thinking that they are ensured of a place in heaven on the back of some long-ago event which the evidence makes clear has made absolutely no difference to their relationship with God.

But the Bible makes clear that all true believers have been, are being, and will be saved. Salvation is an experience in three tenses! The present evidence of saving faith is that it is enduring, demonstrated in a life of principled obedience and genuine and growing godliness. This is not the inevitable preservation of those who live as they please with the false confidence of some notional get-out-of-hell-free card. This is the perseverance of the saints—the confidence of those who pursue that holiness without which no one will see the Lord (Hebrews 12:14). That yoking together of a life of holiness and the hope of heaven should never be overlooked.

True and healthy believers are those who embrace the purposes of God, rest on the promises of God, accept the providences of God, rejoice in the provisions of God, and obey the precepts of God, trusting in and clinging to his person as revealed in Christ Jesus:

> And you, who once were alienated and enemies in your mind by wicked works, yet now He has reconciled in the body of His flesh through death, to present you holy, and blameless, and above reproach in His sight—if indeed you continue in the faith, grounded and steadfast, and are not moved away from the hope of the gospel which you heard, which was preached to every creature under heaven, of which I, Paul, became a minister. (Colossians 1:21–23)

This is a life of real godliness, for it is not the one who lives carnally and casually who lasts the course, but only the one who—even in the face of the world's hatred and despite the growing coolness of heart of many who profess to follow Christ—actively and carefully endures to the end who shall be saved (Matthew 10:22, 24:13).

We were not chosen to drift along on the world's current and be guaranteed that we would reach harbor at last. We were chosen to be holy (Ephesians 1:4), to wrestle on toward heaven against storm and wind and tide.[9]

This being so, "we must give the more earnest heed to the things we have heard, lest we drift away" (Hebrews 2:1). We must beware lest we fall from our own steadfastness; we must set out to grow in the grace and knowledge of Christ Jesus (1 Peter 2:17–18). When God's people hear even the soberest and most chilling warnings of the Bible, they take them to heart, and so flee wickedness. The righteous man holds to his way and presses on in godliness (Job 17:9). Trusting in the Lord his God, the righteous man is held fast, and so holds fast (Psalm 125:1–2).

Neglect of the means that God has provided for the saints to stand fast is a fearful prophecy of drifting, even damage. Such neglect is a threat of ultimate destruction for those who prove that, despite appearances, Christ never knew them. Whatever they might have boasted, they practiced lawlessness and so have no place in Christ's realm now or eternally (Matthew 7:23, 13:41).

These realities are to be used and not abused. Using them wisely reveals spiritual substance in the life of a child of God. Abusing them foolishly makes clear the spiritual vacuum in the heart of a hypocrite. The people of God, saved by Christ, indwelled by the Spirit, shall endure to the end. They shall prove more than conquerors through him who loved us (Romans 8:37).

Thankfulness. How these things should stir us to *thankfulness* for divine grace and faithfulness! The

God who planned this work from before the foundation of the world, and who has begun this good work in us, will complete it. He himself has said that he will never leave us or forsake us. If God is for us, who can be against us? All these sweet truths ought to stir the heart to thankful joy.

Encouragement. But how much *encouragement* is also found here? Perhaps some readers have never come to Christ because they fear they cannot keep with him. That is much like a drowning man refusing to trust the lifeguard because the drowning man cannot swim. But that is the whole point! Finding nothing in ourselves, no strength or wisdom by means of which to obtain or maintain our salvation, we come to Christ to save and keep us, providing all required by every one of his people. He will save us, and he will keep us saved to the end by all necessary means and giving all needful grace.

Discernment. This calls for *discernment*: have you come to this Christ? Have you heard his voice and followed him? Many people make very bold claims for themselves or on behalf of others, but here is a key question: are you living a life of righteousness as one responding to the gracious call and gospel commands of the Lord Jesus, or are you disregarding God and his Word? The man or woman, boy or girl, who lives without regard to God and his truth is not a Christian, whatever they may say or demand. If you or someone else do not live as a Christian, then it is a folly and a crime for you, anyone else, and the church of Christ as a whole, to pretend that you are one:

> For a good tree does not bear bad fruit, nor does a bad tree bear good fruit. For every tree is known by its own fruit. For men do not gather figs from thorns, nor do they gather grapes from a bramble bush. A good man out of the good treasure of his heart brings forth good; and an evil man out of the evil treasure of his heart brings forth evil. For out of the abundance of the heart his mouth speaks. (Luke 6:43–45)

Direction. That makes all of this also a matter of *direction*. Sinners must flee to Jesus Christ in order to be saved. Whoever knows that they are lost should come to Christ. Whoever fears that they are lost should come to Christ. Those who doubt and wrestle should cling to Christ. Those who think they stand should hold to Christ, lest they fall. There is no lasting peace or firm assurance far from Christ. A holy, healthy, and happy Christian life is lived close to the cross, entertaining at once the deepest views of sin and the highest views of God and the most expansive views of divine grace in the Son of God.

Exhortation. Here also is a ground of *exhortation*: trust and obey! Hold fast and press on! There is no contradiction between these commands. On the one hand there is the warning of Matthew 7:21–23:

Not everyone who says to Me, "Lord, Lord," shall enter the kingdom of heaven, but he who does the will of My Father in heaven. Many will say to Me in that day, "Lord, Lord, have we not prophesied in Your name, cast out demons in Your name, and done many wonders in Your name?" And then I will declare to them, "I never knew you; depart from Me, you who practice lawlessness!"

Immediately following there is the assurance of Matthew 7:24–25:

Therefore whoever hears these sayings of Mine, and does them, I will liken him to a wise man who built his house on the rock: and the rain descended, the floods came, and the winds blew and beat on that house; and it did not fall, for it was founded on the rock.

These things belong together; they flow into one another; they complement each other. We must build on the rock: the rock is our foundation, and we build upon it. We must look to Christ and live for Christ to the end, working out our own salvation with fear and trembling, for it is God who works in us both to will and to do for his good pleasure (Philippians 2:12–13). Every true child of God must and does, in dependence on Christ's Spirit and as the result of new life in his soul, obey Peter's command:

But also for this very reason, giving all diligence, add to your faith virtue, to virtue knowledge, to knowledge self-control, to self-control perseverance, to perseverance godliness, to godliness brotherly kindness, and to brotherly kindness love. For if these things are yours and abound, you will be neither barren nor unfruitful in the knowledge of our Lord Jesus Christ. For he who lacks these things is shortsighted, even to blindness, and has forgotten that he was cleansed from his old sins. Therefore, brethren, be even more diligent to make your call and election sure, for if you do these things you will never stumble. (2 Peter 1:5–10)

Comfort and hope. Never lose sight, either, of the *comfort and hope* that these truths contain. God will keep his people. We are utterly weak, but he is infinitely strong. We are feebler than we can imagine; God is mightier than we can calculate. His purposes are sure, his promises are true, his providences are wise, his provisions are complete, his precepts are sweet, his person is altogether love.

Praise. And so all comes to *praise* to this great God for his so-great salvation. As we consider the plan of his redeeming love we find before us a display of grace from beginning to end. There is no part of our salvation that is not rooted in, prompted by, and awash in God's free favor. God's grace in Christ underpins each element and undergirds each step. Christians are being, have been, and will be saved to the praise of God's glorious grace (Ephesians 1:6, 12, 14). No Christian committed to the glory of God above all else would have it any other way. Indeed, such a man as John Owen, the great Puritan pastor and preacher, can even say that it is "better we should all eternally come short of forgiveness than that God should lose anything of his glory."[10]

Is that the testimony of your heart? The wonder of it is that God's glory and his people's good are not at odds with one another. Grace binds the two together, so that my good is secured to his glory and his glory is displayed in my good. Salvation is of the Lord, entirely and completely, and yet it is a salvation that draws out and engages all that I am and have. God's salvation brings me from the depths of hell to the heights of heaven, and all in a display of grace that adorns the character of God, revealing the majesty of Christ, and secures the honor of the eternal and triune Name.

> Now to Him who is able to keep you from stumbling,
> And to present you faultless
> Before the presence of His glory with exceeding joy,
> To God our Savior,
> Who alone is wise,
> Be glory and majesty,
> Dominion and power,
> Both now and forever. Amen. (Jude 24–25)

This puts a song in the heart and on the lips of the saints through time and to all eternity:

> After these things I looked, and behold, a great multitude which no one could number, of all nations, tribes, peoples, and tongues, standing before the throne and before the Lamb, clothed with white robes, with palm branches in their hands, and crying out with a loud voice, saying, "Salvation belongs to our God who sits on the throne, and to the Lamb!" All the angels stood around the throne and the elders and the four living creatures, and fell on their faces before the throne and worshiped God, saying:
>
> "Amen!
> Blessing and glory and wisdom,
> Thanksgiving and honor and power and might,
> Be to our God forever and ever.
> Amen." (Revelation 7:9–12)

Author

Jeremy Walker was born to godly parents and was converted to Christ during his teenage years. He serves as a pastor of Maidenbower Baptist Church, Crawley, England, and is married to Alissa, with whom he enjoys the blessing of three children. He has written several books and has blogged at Reformation21 and The Wanderer.

Endnotes

1. William Gurnall, *The Christian in Complete Armour* (Edinburgh: Banner of Truth, 1964, repr. 1989), 1:230.
2. Thomas Boston, *Human Nature in its Fourfold State* (Edinburgh: Banner of Truth, 1964, repr. 1997), 57 ff.
3. "In Stetson or Wig, He's Hard to Pin Down," by Sarah Lyall, *New York Times*, November 4, 2007, http://www.nytimes.com/2007/11/04/movies/moviesspecial/04lyal.html, accessed 5/11/2015.
4. From the hymn, "When I Survey the Wondrous Cross" by Isaac Watts.
5. From the hymn, "I Lift My Heart to Thee, Saviour Divine" by Charles E. Mudie.
6. *The Shorter Catechism: A Baptist Version* (Avinger, TX: Simpson Publishing Company, 1991), 14.
7. William O'Neill, "The Final Perseverance of Believers in Christ Jesus" in *Exposition of the Doctrines of Grace* (Pasadena, TX: Pilgrim Publications, 1861), 323.
8. O'Neill, "The Final Perseverance," 328.
9. The sentiment is from Anne Ross Cousin's hymn, "The Sands of Time are Sinking," based on Samuel Rutherford's prose.
10. John Owen, *The Works of John Owen*, ed. William H. Goold, vol. 6 (Edinburgh: T&T Clark, n.d.), 403.

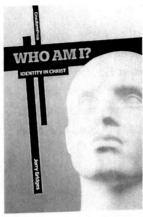

Who Am I?
Identity in Christ

by Jerry Bridges

Jerry Bridges unpacks Scripture to give the Christian eight clear, simple, interlocking answers to one of the most essential questions of life.

91 pages
bit.ly/WHOAMI

"Jerry Bridges' gift for simple but deep spiritual communication is fully displayed in this warm-hearted, biblical spelling out of the Christian's true identity in Christ."
> **J.I. Packer, Theological Editor, ESV Study Bible; author, Knowing God, A Quest for Godliness, Concise Theology**

"I know of no one better prepared than Jerry Bridges to write *Who Am I?* He is a man who knows who he is in Christ and he helps us to see succinctly and clearly who we are to be. Thank you for another gift to the Church of your wisdom and insight in this book."
> **R.C. Sproul, founder, chairman, president, Ligonier Ministries; executive editor, Tabletalk magazine; general editor, The Reformation Study Bible**

"*Who Am I?* answers one of the most pressing questions of our time in clear gospel categories straight from the Bible. This little book is a great resource to ground new believers and remind all of us of what God has made us through faith in Jesus. Thank the Lord for Jerry Bridges, who continues to provide the warm, clear, and biblically balanced teaching that has made him so beloved to this generation of Christians."
> **Richard D. Phillips, Senior Minister, Second Presbyterian Church, Greenville, SC**

WHO AM I? (Excerpts...in smaller type than usual!)

INTRODUCTION

Who are you?

- The man sitting to my left at a dinner referred to himself as a carpenter. Carpentry is his vocation, but it is not who he is.
- A lady with a broken marriage said to a friend, "I am just a failure." Although she had failed in her marriage, that is not who she is.
- I grew up in moderate poverty. To this day, my default answer to the question, "Who am I?" is, "I am the little boy growing up on the dirt street alongside the railroad track." But that is not who I am.

These three responses illustrate the common tendency to answer the question "Who am I?" in terms of some subjective experience. Many of us answer in terms of our vocation. Others focus on a particularly formative or emotional experience.

I serve with the Navigators collegiate ministry, primarily focusing on staff development. But I am familiar enough with the student scene to know that many young people arrive at college from difficult family backgrounds, or carrying the baggage of their own sinful lifestyles during their high school days. As a result, many of them have low or even negative self-images. Many, if honest, would answer the question "Who am I?" in terms of their negative or sinful experiences.

As Christians, however, our identity is to be found in our relationship with Christ, not in our subjective and often negative life experiences. In our ministry to students, therefore, we seek to help them become aware of their "position and identity in Christ," so that their answer to the question "Who am I?" is based on what it means to be "in Christ."

There is no short and simple answer to the question, "Who am I in Christ?" That position involves both privileges and responsibilities. It involves some tremendously astounding truths about us, but also faces us with some sobering facts that are just as true.

In this book we are going to look at eight different answers to the question, "Who am I?" It is my prayer that these eight answers will give us a balanced, biblical view of what it means to be in Christ.

CHAPTER TWO: I AM IN CHRIST

We have begun to answer the question "Who am I?" with the fact that we are all creatures, created in the image of God, dependent on him, and accountable to him. This is true of everyone born into the world whether we realize it or not. But for those of us who have trusted in Christ as our Savior, there is much more to our identity than simply being creatures.

The answer to the question, "Who am I as a Christian?", is far more elaborate and wonderful than the answer to the simpler (if still profound) question, "Who am I as a human being?" Once we are converted, there are seven additional glorious truths that come into play as essential components of our identity. These will constitute our focus for the remainder of this book.

As we seek to answer that more elaborate question, it is beyond dispute that we must start with the fact that we are "in" Christ Jesus.

What does it mean to be in Christ? Is it a question of location, like being in a house? Is it something like belonging to a club or an organization? No, the term "in Christ" is the apostle Paul's shorthand expression for being united to Christ. It is one of Paul's favorite expressions, and (including similar expressions such as "in him" or "in the Lord") Paul uses it more than 160 times in his letters. Clearly this is an important concept in Paul's theology. And it should be an important concept for us because *all the remaining answers to the question "Who am I?" are based upon the fact that we are in Christ, or we are united to Christ.*

This of course begs the question, what does it mean to be united to Christ? To answer it, we begin with 1 Corinthians 15:22, "For as in Adam all die, so also in Christ shall all be made alive." Note the two expressions "in Adam" and "in Christ." And again in 1 Corinthians 15:45, Paul refers to "the first man Adam" and to "the last Adam," who is clearly Christ. What Paul is getting at in these two verses is that in God's way of dealing with humanity there are only two men, Adam and Christ. *All the rest of us are represented before God by one or the other of these two men.*

Adam as Our Representative

In verse 22 Paul said, "in Adam all die." This idea is developed more completely in Romans 5:12-19. Verse 12 says, "Therefore, just as sin came into the world through one man, and death through sin, and so death spread to all men because all sinned...." This verse is a reference to Adam's sin of eating the forbidden fruit as recounted in Genesis 3. God had said, "but of the tree of the knowledge of good and evil you shall not eat, for in the day that you eat of it you shall surely die." Adam, along with Eve, ate, and they both died. They instantly died spiritually, and they would eventually die physically. But Adam was not an ordinary man so that the consequences of his sin would fall only on him.

Rather, Adam had been appointed by God to represent the entire human race. As a result, the consequences of his sin fell upon all humanity. When Paul writes in verse 12, "and so death spread to all men because all sinned...," he is referring, not to our own individual sins, but to the fact that we were so united to Adam as our representative head that when he sinned we all sinned, and so we all suffered the consequences of Adam's sin.

This idea of the representative nature of Adam's sin is further developed in verse 18, "Therefore, as one trespass led to condemnation for all men," and again in verse 19, "For as by the one man's disobedience the many were made sinners." Note especially in verse 19 the expression, "many were made sinners." All humanity (with the exception of Christ, who was not descended from Adam) suffered the consequences of Adam's sin. We were *made* sinners. As each of us comes into the world, we come as sinners by nature.

In answer to the question "Who am I?" we would therefore have to say, "I am a sinner." That is why David acknowledged, "Surely I was sinful at birth, sinful from the time my mother conceived me" (Psalms 51:5 NIV). David said the nature he received at conception was a sinful nature. Why was this true? It was because David, like you and me, was represented by Adam in the garden, and through the disobedience of Adam, David was made a sinner.

Picture two men, Adam and Christ, standing before God. Behind Adam stands all of humanity representatively united to him. We all come into this world "in Adam." Because of that, Paul's descriptive words in Ephesians 2:1-3 are true of every one of us before we trust Christ. Here is what he wrote:

And you were dead in the trespasses and sins in which you once walked, following the course of this world, following the prince of the power of the air, the spirit that is now at work in the sons of disobedience-- among whom we all once lived in the passions of our flesh, carrying out the desires of the body and the mind, and were by nature children of wrath, like the rest of mankind.

Paul's description of our dismal condition can be summed up in three expressions:

- Spiritually dead
- Slaves (to the world, the devil, and our sinful passions)
- Objects of God's wrath

Think of that! As one "in Adam" you came into the world an object of God's wrath. It doesn't matter whether we were born of Christian parents or pagan parents. We are all born "in Adam" and so an object of God's wrath. All because Adam sinned.

Not only all of humanity, but creation itself suffered the consequences of Adam's sin. Though in Genesis 3:17-19, God refers specifically to cursing the ground, Paul in Romans 8:19-22, speaks of the futility of all creation. So we all come into the world spiritually dead, objects of God's wrath, and into a natural environment that is under the curse of God. That is what it means to be "in Adam."

Christ as Our Representative

The other man standing before God is the "last Adam," namely the Lord Jesus Christ. Just as God appointed Adam to represent all of humanity, so he appointed Christ to represent all who trust in him as Savior. We have looked at the consequences of Adam's representative act in Romans 5:18-19. Now observe the contrasting effects of Christ's work on behalf of all who trust in him. Verse 18: "so one act of righteousness leads to justification and life for all men." And in verse 19, "so by the one man's obedience the many will be made righteous."

For the sake of clarity, we need to draw out Paul's artful use of language in verses 18 and 19.

- Verse 18: "as one trespass led to condemnation for all men, so one act of righteousness leads to justification and life for all men." In this verse, the first appearance of "all men" refers to our universal condemnation. The second appearance refers to the universal offer of salvation, not the universal existence of salvation. There is universal condemnation, and there is a universal way of escape, yet not all will escape.

- Verse 19: "For as by the one man's disobedience the many were made sinners, so by the one man's obedience the many will be made righteous." Here, Paul follows the same artful use of language as in verse 18. The first appearance of "the many" is a universal statement, while the second appearance refers exclusively to those who come to Christ.

In each verse, therefore, the first "all" and "many" refer to the fact that all humanity has suffered the consequences of Adam's sin. The second "all" and "many" refer only to all those who trust in Christ and are "in him."

What are the results of being in him? We will explore these in detail in subsequent chapters, but for now I want to call our attention to the principle by which God operates.

Obedience and Disobedience

In Deuteronomy 28, Moses sets before the nation of Israel two alternatives: obedience and disobedience. The results of obedience are tremendous blessings. The results of disobedience are horrible curses. These particular blessings and curses are all temporal in nature and refer specifically to the nation of Israel in the Promised Land. But at the same time they are an expression of the eternal principle by which God operates: blessings for obedience and curses for disobedience.

By his perfectly obedient life over thirty-three years, Christ earned the blessings of God. By his death on the cross he experienced the curse for disobedience. As our representative, all that he did in both his life and death accrues to our benefit. Someone has said it like this: "He lived the life we could not live, and died the death we deserved to die." Or again, "He was treated as we deserved to be treated in order that we might be treated as he deserved to be treated."

When we think of the work of Christ, we usually think of his death to pay for our sin. We call this his "substitutionary atonement," in that he died in our place, as our substitute, to satisfy the justice of God for our sins. But what is it that makes this substitution valid? How could God's justice be satisfied when a perfectly innocent man suffers punishment on behalf of those who actually deserve it?

The answer is that Christ stood before God as our representative. He assumed the responsibility for our obedience to the law of God, *and* he assumed the responsibility to render to God satisfaction for our disobedience. All this because we are "in him," that is, we are united to him in a representative way.

The Living Union

This truth of Christ's representative union with us is foundational to all that we will be considering in subsequent chapters as we seek to answer the question, "Who am I?" But there is also a whole other dimension of our union with Christ that is equally exciting and that will help us understand who we are. That is what we call our living union with Christ.

This living union is best explained by Jesus' use of the vine and branch metaphor in John 15:1-5. Just as the branch shares in the life and nourishment of the vine, so we as believers share in the life of Christ. This living union is affected by the Holy Spirit who lives within us (See 1 Corinthians 6:19-20), and who imparts to us the spiritual vitality of Christ himself.

As a young Christian I did not realize what it meant to be in a living union with Christ. My concept of my relationship to Christ was that he was in heaven and I was on earth. To me, prayer was like a long distance phone call to heaven, in which I might get through or I might not. My Christian life was largely one of self-effort.

One day in a time of discouragement I said to myself, "How can someone in Christ be as discouraged as I am?" At the time I had no idea of what it meant to be in Christ. To me it was just another expression for being a Christian. But as soon as I said those words, the thought came into my mind, (planted, I think, by the Holy Spirit), "What did you just say? What does it mean to be in Christ?"

So I went to my favorite place to spend time alone with God and began to ponder the question, "What does it mean to be in Christ?" I had memorized various verses which had in them the words "in Christ," or "in him" or "in the Lord," but as I said, the words had no special meaning for me. But that day, as those verses began to flow through my mind, I saw the truth in John 15:1-5 that I had a vital living relationship with Christ. I was actually a partaker of his life. I didn't need to make long-distance calls to heaven. No, I was in him, and through his Spirit he was in me.

Of all the Scriptures that went through my mind that morning, the most exciting to me was 1 Corinthians 1:30 which in the King James Version says, "But of him are ye in Christ Jesus, who of God is made unto us wisdom, and righteousness, and sanctification, and redemption." The thought that was so exciting to me was that it is *of God* that I am in Christ Jesus. I didn't, as it were, get into Christ of my own doing. It was God who united me to him. It was by his action that I am in Christ Jesus.

Isn't that encouraging? God is the one who unites us to Christ.

To use Paul's expression, he is the one who has placed us in Christ. That means we can never get out. We didn't do anything to get in, and we can't do anything to get out. It's all of God.

Even today, fifty-five years later, that verse brings sparkle to my life. I often wake up discouraged about something. But as I get dressed and walk down the hall to the kitchen to make a cup of coffee, 1 Corinthians 1:30 will come to my mind and I say to myself, "God, it is of you that I am in Christ." And all of a sudden I will break into a great big smile, and the discouragement is gone.

The idea that our being in Christ is all of God, and further, because we are in Christ, his very life flows into us, could lead to the impression that we have no responsibility or part to play in this relationship. First of all, although it is indeed of God that we are united to Christ, we are united to him *by faith*. But where do we get the faith? It is the gift of God (See Ephesians 2:8-9 and Acts 16:14). But though this faith is given to us, we must still exercise it.

Having exercised faith to believe in Christ, we must also exercise faith to draw upon the life and nourishment that comes to us from Christ through our living union with him. There are some who teach that just as the branch does nothing to receive the nourishment of the vine, so we do nothing to receive the life and energy of Christ. But this presses the analogy too far. Just as Christ is not entirely like a vine, we are not entirely like branches. Human beings are unique in that we have been created in the image of God. He has, among other things, given us minds to think with and wills which we may exercise, and he works through our minds and wills; not apart from them.

So in summary, we see that there are two related but distinct aspects of being in Christ, that is, united to him.

Representative union. The first is the representative union by which Jesus assumed all our responsibility to perfectly obey the law of God, and also assumed our penalty of death for not obeying. We will explore the results of this in the next two chapters.

Living union. The second aspect is the living union through the Holy Spirit, by which we, by faith, draw upon the nourishment and power of the living Christ to enable us to live the Christian life.

Further development of these two aspects will help us to answer the question, "Who am I?"

By the work of God, I am no longer in Adam:
I am in Christ, through a union that is both living and representative.

Knowable Word
Helping Ordinary People Learn to Study the Bible

by Peter Krol
Foreword by Tedd Tripp

Observe...Interpret...Apply

Simple concepts at the heart of good Bible study. Learn the basics in a few minutes—gain skills for a lifetime. The spiritual payoff is huge...ready?

108 pages   bit.ly/Knowable

"Peter Krol has done us a great service by writing the book Knowable Word. It is valuable for those who have never done in-depth Bible study and a good review for those who have. I look forward to using this book to improve my own Bible study.'"

Jerry Bridges, author, The Pursuit of Holiness, and many more

"It is hard to over-estimate the value of this tidy volume. It is clear and uncomplicated. No one will be off-put by this book. It will engage the novice and the serious student of Scripture. It works as a solid read for individuals or as an exciting study for a small group."

Tedd Tripp, pastor and author (from the Foreword)

"At the heart of *Knowable Word* is a glorious and crucial conviction: that understanding the Bible is not the preserve of a few, but the privilege and joy of all God's people. Peter Krol's book demystifies the process of reading God's Word and in so doing enfranchises the people of God. I warmly encourage you to read it.."

Dr. Tim Chester, The Porterbrook Network

"Here is an excellent practical guide to interpreting the Bible. Krol has thought through, tested, and illustrated in a clear, accessible way basic steps in interpreting the Bible, and made everything available in a way that will encourage ordinary people to deepen their own study."

Vern Poythress, Westminster Theological Seminary

JOY! – A Bible Study on
Philippians for Women

bit.ly/JoyStudy

FAITH: A Bible Study on
James for Women

bit.ly/FaithStudy

Inductive Bible studies for women by Keri Folmar
endorsed by...

Kathleen Nielson is author of the *Living Word Bible Studies*; Director
of Women's Initiatives, The Gospel Coalition; and wife of Niel,
who served as President of Covenant College from 2002 to 2012.

Diane Schreiner – wife of professor, author, and pastor Tom Schreiner,
and mother of four grown children – has led women's Bible
studies for more than 20 years.

Connie Dever is author of *The Praise Factory* children's ministry
curriculum and wife of Pastor Mark Dever, President of 9 Marks
Ministries

Kristie Anyabwile, holds a history degree from NC State University,
and is married to Thabiti, Senior Pastor of First Baptist Church,
Grand Cayman, and a Council Member for The Gospel
Coalition.

Gloria Furman is a pastor's wife in the Middle East and author of
Glimpses of Grace and *Treasuring Christ When Your Hands Are Full.*

The Company We Keep
In Search of Biblical Friendship

by Jonathan Holmes
Foreword by Ed Welch

Biblical friendship is deep, honest, pure, tranparent, and liberating.

It is also attainable.

112 pages
bit.ly/B-Friend

"Jonathan Holmes has the enviable ability to say a great deal in a few words. Here is a wonderful primer on the nature of biblical friendship—what it means and why it matters."
Alistair Begg, Truth for Life; Senior Pastor, Parkside Church

"Jonathan has succeeded in giving us a picture of how normal, daily, biblical friend-ships can be used by God to mold us into the likeness of Christ. If you want a solid, fresh way of re-thinking all of your relationships, read this book."
Dr. Tim S. Lane, co-author, How People Change

"A robust and relevant GPS for intentional and vulnerable gospel-centered friendships...a great book not only for individuals, but also for small groups...a signifi-cant contribution to the Kingdom."
Robert W. Kellemen, Exec. Dir., Biblical Counseling Coalition

"Short. Thoughtful. Biblical. Practical. I'm planning to get my friends to read this book so we can transform our friendships."
Deepak Reju, Pastor of Biblical Counseling, Capitol Hill Baptist

"Filled with answers that are equally down-to-earth, nitty-gritty, and specific...taking us where we need to go with warmth and wisdom."
Wesley Hill, author, Washed and Waiting

"But God..."
The Two Words at the Heart of the Gospel

by Casey Lute

Just two words.
Understand their use in Scripture,
and you will never be the same.

100 pages
bit.ly/ButGOD

"Keying off of nine occurrences of "But God" in the English Bible, Casey Lute ably opens up Scripture in a manner that is instructive, edifying, encouraging, and convicting. This little book would be useful in family or personal reading, or as a gift to a friend. You will enjoy Casey's style, you will have a fresh view of some critical Scripture, and your appreciation for God's mighty grace will be deepened."
> **Dan Phillips, Pyromaniacs blog, author of The World-Tilting Gospel (forthcoming from Kregel)**

"A refreshingly concise, yet comprehensive biblical theology of grace that left this reader more in awe of the grace of God. "
> **Aaron Armstrong, BloggingTheologically.com**

""Casey Lute reminds us that nothing is impossible with God, that we must always reckon with God, and that God brings life out of death and joy out of sorrow. "
> **Thomas R. Schreiner, Professor of New Testament Interpretation, The Southern Baptist Theological Seminary**

"A mini-theology that will speak to the needs of every reader of this small but powerful book. Read it yourself and you will be blessed. Give it to a friend and you will be a blessing."
> **William Varner, Prof. of Biblical Studies, The Master's College**

The Most Encouraging Book on Hell Ever

by Thor Ramsey

The biblical view of hell is under attack. But if hell freezes over, we lose a God of love and holiness, the good new of Jesus Christ, and more.

This book was written because hell glorifies God.

97 pages   bit.ly/HELLBOOK

"Is the fear of God merely an Old-Testament doctrine? Does hell glorify God? Will we party with Pol Pot, Vlad the Impaler, Stalin, the Marquis de Sade, and Satan in heaven? And what about Bill Maher? For answers to these and other questions, this thought-provoking, bracing corrective to the soapy bromides of recent volumes on this subject may be just the ticket. And have we mentioned that it's entertaining and encouraging?"

> ***Eric Metaxas, New York Times Best-selling author of*
> Bonhoeffer: Pastor, Martyr, Prophet, Spy**

"*The Most Encouraging Book on Hell Ever* is also one of the wisest. This book is crammed with hilarious quips, but the message is deadly serious. Losing the doctrine of hell isn't trivial. It means losing truth, righteousness, and grace. Ultimately it means losing God. Thor's book uses humor to disarm readers just enough to deliver this crucial and timely message."

> ***Drew Dyck, managing editor of* Leadership Journal, *a*
> Christianity Today *publication***

"'Praise God for Thor! The end must be getting near as Christians are actually getting funny. After a few pages, you'll realize this ain't your grandma's book about hell... but she'd love it just the same. Because it's only funny in the right places."

> ***Stephen Baldwin, actor, author, radio host***

The Two Fears
Tremble Before God Alone

by Chris Poblete

**You can fear God...
or everything else.**

**Only one fear brings life and hope,
wisdom and joy.**

Fear wisely.

92 pages   bit.ly/2Fears

"We are too scared. And we aren't scared enough. Reading this book
will prompt you to seek in your own life the biblical tension between
'fear not' and 'fear God.'"
Russell D. Moore, Dean, Southern Baptist Theological Seminary

"An importantly counter-cultural book, moving us beyond a
homeboy God we could fist-bump to a holy God we can worship.
The Two Fears helps us recover a biblical fear of God and all the awe,
repentance, and freedom from self-centered fears that go with it. An
awesome resource!"
Dr. Thaddeus Williams, professor, Biola University

"In this practical and very readable book, Chris Poblete shows how
both the absence of true fear and the presence of 'unholy [false] fear'
stem from an absence of a knowledge of the awesome God of the
Bible, and that, in meeting him, we discover the real dimensions of
creational existence and the wonderful benefits of living in fear and
deep respect before him, freed from the '[false] fear of men.'"
*Peter Jones, Ph.D., TruthXchange; Scholar-in-Residence and
Adjunct Professor, Westminster Seminary in California*

"I commend this book to you: it will fuel your worship and empower
your discipleship."
Gabe Tribbett, Christ's Covenant Church, Winona Lake, IA

Good News About Satan
A Gospel Look at Spiritual Warfare

by Bob Bevington
Foreword by Jerry Bridges

The world, the flesh...the Devil and his demons. How do they work together against us?

Learn to recognize and resist the enemy in the power of the gopel.

108 pages   bit.ly/SATANLOSES

"Spiritual warfare is certainly an important biblical topic; from one perspective it is the central topic of the whole Bible. So it's important that believers get sober and reliable guidance on the subject. Bob Bevington's book is one of the most helpful. His book is reliable, biblical, and practical. It is easy to understand and challenges our spiritual complacency."
Dr. John M. Frame, Reformed Theological Seminary

"This is the best book I have ever read on this subject. I simply could not put it down. It is both highly Christ-centered and very practical, having the wonderful effect of focusing the reader's attention directly on Jesus while at the same time providing much useful help in the believer's battle against the enemy."
Mike Cleveland, Founder and President, Setting Captives Free

"Filled with biblical reconnaissance and helpful insights for the conduct of spiritual warfare... a stimulating analysis of the biblical data, drawing boundaries between the factual and fanciful, and grounding the reader firmly on the gospel of Jesus Christ."
Stanley Gale, author, What is Spiritual Warfare?

"Read this book, prepare for battle, and rejoice in the victory that has been won and the glory that will shine more brightly."
Justin Taylor, co-author, The Final Days of Jesus

CPSIA information can be obtained
at www.ICGtesting.com
Printed in the USA
FFOW05n0533090616